# INDOOR PLANTS

# INDOOR PLANTS

## BY XENIA FIELD

HAMLYN

First published in 1966
Published by
The Hamlyn Publishing Group Limited,
Hamlyn House, Feltham, Middlesex, England
© Xenia Field, 1966
Third Impression 1970
Printed in Czechoslovakia by PZ, Bratislava
ISBN 0 600 01992 6
52025/2

FRONTISPIECE
*An attractive arrangement consisting of:* HEDERA CANA-
RIENSIS, CARRAGUATA, TRADESCANTIA, FITTONIA VER-
SCHAEFELTII, CYCLAMEN SILVER LEAF *and* KEUBIA PALM.

# CONTENTS

# INTRODUCTION

Indoor gardening is an absorbing pursuit — as popular with coalminers and footballers as with the aged and the invalid.

The house-plant grower may fairly boast that he is 200 years ahead of the conservatory gardener. He can proudly point to St. Ursula's Vision by Carpaccio, painted about the year 1500; the lady certainly has two pots in her window and she was unlikely to be the only horticulturist of her day.

Conservatories, on the other hand, did not make their appearance until the 17th century.

There is also evidence that the early civilisations, Roman, Egyptian and Indian, had pots and tubs in plenty and, no doubt, brought some of them into their homes.

As the famous Mr Middleton once told me, some thousand species of plants had, to his knowledge, been grown indoors and I am sure many more succulents and others would welcome the opportunity.

Meanwhile, the popularity of pots in rooms is spreading, although certain plants come and go with fashion. The musk, which has grown in jardinière and cottage window alike, lost popularity when it mislaid its scent and is now scarcely seen at all; but the rubber plant is to be seen almost everywhere.

Indoor gardening requires experience and skill. When I'd presented a prize to an old lady in the provinces who had kept her emerald feather, Asparagus Sprengeri, for a quarter of a century in her front room — a great feat — she said, "We're both champion!"

This is as it should be, plants must be in 'champion' order to be satisfying. It is not enough to keep a plant alive, for a sickly plant is an ugly sight.

I hope this book will help you to keep leaves the right green, the plant vigorous, buds bursting — and you a proud gardener.

# PART ONE

# CHOOSING A PLANT

We are beginning to know our house plants — more important still, they are beginning to know us. The understanding owner has learnt that he must keep his *aphelandra* moist, provide humidity for his cyclamen and African Violet, and fulfil the special requirements of the more difficult customers.

Meanwhile, the plants, even the more temperamental of them, are playing their part by doing their best to acclimatize themselves to our homes and the unskilled hands of the amateur.

The last ten years have indeed been a testing time during which, thousands and thousands of plants must have died unhappy, mouldy deaths. But at long last we have, to a great extent, mastered the art of growing plants in our homes. The first step was to draw the dividing line between the stove (heated greenhouse) and the house plant.

I always describe the indoor plant as one that consents to become, with cheerful tolerance, the willing, happy and permanent inhabitant of a normal home.

The real indoor plant should be able to adapt itself, as we ourselves do, to the room conditions of a house or flat. There may be a coal fire or artificial heat, the window will be opened on occasion and the temperature will rise and fall in a comfortable or uncomfortable manner.

The plant that resents house conditions and is constantly hankering for the humidity and steady temperature of the greenhouse is a depressing companion and obviously not for the house. Unless you are prepared to acclimatize yourself to more tropical surroundings it is wise to confine your gardening to those plants which are prepared to accept your home as it is, with perhaps mild modifications.

Knowing how to buy is, in its way, as important as knowing how to grow and one of the main purposes of this book is to help the beginner to buy the right plant for his particular room. He must beware of stove plants such as the poinsettia or gloxinia, for the gardener who crosses the boundary between 'house' and 'stove' plants does so at his own risk. To introduce a *columnea gloriosa* into a cold room would make it so unutterably miserable that its owner would be quite relieved when it passed out.

You cannot be expected to change your home to suit plants, but at least you can choose plants to suit your home.

I ask gardeners to grade themselves as beginners, graduates and greenfingers, and not to tackle the more temperamental subjects until they have mastered the easy ones. Mr. Thomas Rochford has now gone a step further in this direction by labelling his plants, *easy*, *intermediate* or *delicate*. If you listen to us both you should not find the task of buying difficult.

However, there will always be those who insist on growing roses although they live in a swamp, those who *must* grow the Himalayan rhododendron, native of the tree-shaded mountains, even if they have only sun-baked limestone to offer. Maybe they never heard of Reginald Arkell's warning:

> 'A rhododendron set in lime
> Looks like a curate doing time.'

▶ BEGONIA TOSCA.

Nurserymen are only too familiar with the *must* gardeners, who put the peat-lovers on lime and tuck the lime-lovers in peat. Now they are meeting those who *must* have African Violets in a room where the water-jug freezes at night or crotons from Malay at the mercy of a whistling draught.

Don't take the hard road. Don't send your plant to the grave!

If you live in a cold place or if you are away a great deal and the heating is turned off, then you must call upon the truly hardy (see Part 2). Only they are likely to stand up to it. Again, if all heating is turned off at night, the very temperamental should be avoided.

If you live in a dark room without sun, you must choose a non-flowering plant; although many foliage

plants can manage without the sun, very few plants can flower without it.

If the light is poor you must grow shade-lovers (see page 130) and when buying a plant for the bathroom or kitchen, get one that will enjoy the humidity. Where there are gas fumes, choose a *ficus philodendron* or *hedera*, as they are indifferent to a whiff or two. If you live in a draught, and some people do, then it has to be not merely a hardy but a 'toughie' (see Part 2).

The size of the plant should be suitable. The small cactus in a Tom Thumb pot on the grand piano is out of place.

Lastly choose a plant according to your skill as a gardener. Too many beginners start their plant career with an African Violet which is a difficult customer. The beginner should keep to the cast-iron plants (see Part 2), moving up to those for graduates (see Part 3), after which he will be able to tackle the list allocated to green-fingers (see Part 4).

Keep an open mind when you go plant shopping. Listen to the nurseryman, remembering that he will as a rule make the plant's culture sound just a little easier than it is. If you don't over estimate your skill or insist on having a particular plant when you have not the conditions it demands, bit by bit you will become an indoor gardener.

**Tools**

The house plant gardener does not require a toolshed, so the few implements he needs will be largely a matter of his own choice. They must include a sharp knife, a fork of kinds (possibly the old two-prong

◀ TRADESCANTIA.

kitchen variety), preferably with prongs slightly blunted for keeping the soil open, a trowel for planting troughs and large containers, a small secateur for pruning, a fine-nozzled syringe, a potting stick or dibble for planting, and a suitable watering can. This should have a thin spout so that the gardener can direct the water beneath the foliage and keep the moisture away from the vulnerable crown or centre of the plants. A teapot will come in handy at times.

Finally a basket is desirable; it will hold the tools and make for tidiness.

## Arrival

The majority of house plants come to us from the nurseryman's greenhouse either direct or via the florist. They will take a little time to acclimatize themselves to your way of life and are likely to lose a few leaves in the process. The rhythm of growth has been temporarily checked by changed surroundings and who knows what disturbance the plants suffered on the journey.

If a plant arrives dry, give it a good soak of tepid water and leave it to dry out somewhere warm, well out of the draught and full sun. The newcomer should be watched carefully for the first four weeks or so until it has settled down and shown signs of growth.

Whenever possible, acquire your plant in the summer, when the change-over from greenhouse to room is less drastic. If the plant cannot be introduced during the summer, buy it in the autumn, before the heating system is turned on or fires lighted.

▲ PEPEROMIA MAGNOLIAEFOLIA — *a plant suitable for the graduate.*

▼ A SELECTION OF HOUSE PLANTS.

# THREE VITAL FACTORS
# IN GROWING HOUSE PLANTS

## Air and Temperature

Fresh air may not be as vital to a plant as it is to us, but it is a necessity, because of its moisture. High temperatures that rob the air of humidity are the cause of many plant troubles.

Ventilation must therefore be given. Windows are far better opened from the top.

Account should be taken that the nearer the plant to the ceiling, the drier and hotter the air will be. In an overheated or stuffy room a plant is happier just above floor level. The gardener should aim at keeping the room at a temperature of 60—70°F. during the day, falling to 50—60°F. at night. Many of the hardies survive a temperature of 45°F.: the temperamental flinch at temperatures below 55°F. Extremes are harmful, and the differences between day and night temperatures should not be more than 10°F. The plant that is exposed to wide fluctuations (60°F. one day and 80°F. the next, or hot days and freezing nights) will be the first to die. The wet plant is particularly vulnerable.

The desired temperature will depend on whether you intend to grow the hardy, such as the philodendron, or the temperamental, *anthuriums* or *saintpaulias*. Our rooms are often too hot in the wintertime for plant cultivation — a far greater evil than being too cold. There is much to be said for the unheated spare room and it is an ideally peaceful spot for the plant that is resting. But few plants are happy when the temperature consistently falls much below 50°F.

Windows often fit badly and in this event the plants should be moved away from the sill at night or protected by a curtain, newspaper or cardboard screen placed between them and the glass. Care must be taken that the plants are not touched by the frost. If a plant is 'caught', it should be sprayed with cold water and allowed to unstiffen gradually, away from the fire. It may not recover, but you will have done your best to make amends.

Some windows need draught excluders; their introduction tends to improve the health of the gardener, as well as that of his plants.

## Light

Keep your house plants near a window; they require lots of light, for darkness elongates and distorts foliage and bloom, so gloomy corners must be avoided.

Most flowering plants need sunlight if they are to bloom; many foliage plants can manage without the sun but must have light. There are shade-lovers that prefer indirect sunlight and certain degrees of shade.

A number of the hardy and half hardy plants will enjoy a holiday on the window-sill in the sun, full light and rain, during the warm weather.

The pale green, anaemic, limp-leaved specimen usually requires more light, so place it in a west window and watch it perk up. Keep it shaded from a powerful sun until it has regained health.

## Choosing and Tending a Plant

A plant in flower should also be protected from the hot midday sun, otherwise it will be out and over in

▶ HEDERA — *this plant likes a cool light place.*

a jiffy. Pots in windows should be turned round regularly so that the plant that is forever in search of light does not become distorted and lopsided.

Light is a primary need, providing the plant with energy; light and sun mean more flowers. Gay rooms with white or pale walls rather than chocolate or brown paint seem to have an even more cheerful effect upon plants than upon people. Only the mushroom enjoys the dark.

## Artificial Light

The cultivation of plants and bulbs indoors by artificial light has produced encouraging results. Some Dutchmen have been successful in growing daffodils, hyacinths and tulips by artificial light in cellars, and considerable pioneering work is being carried out.

Incandescent bulbs have been replaced in these experiments by fluorescent tubes or strip-lighting that gives more light and less heat, while providing a 16-hour day.

The most satisfactory result that has come my way has been the response of saintpaulia to the warm white tubes of artificial light — this plant needs 14 hours of daylight to bloom freely. The tubes may be positioned in pairs or tiers, 10—11 inches above the plants and the daylight stretch kept to 12—15 hours. The cost is negligible.

Plantariums with fluorescent lighting and reflectors to throw back the illumination, with galvanized trays to hold a pebble base and pots, are useful in a dark corner of the room where there is no daylight.

The gardener should keep in touch with this experimental work that is still in its infancy. The

importance of consulting a professional electrician before taking action, cannot be overstressed. The do-it-yourself method can be dangerous.

## Humidity

The humidity of the air is as important to plant life as constant temperature and light, and is often far more difficult to provide.

Plants other than succulents resent hot, dry rooms. However, the gardener who is prepared to take trouble can increase the moisture of the atmosphere around the plant. In America, enthusiasts go to some pains to provide small water-pans fitted to their radiators to humidify the air. A trough, bowl or tray with small pebbles, gravel, peat or moss, constantly kept moist, will do much the same job. It is important that the arrangement allows a space between the plants and the wall through which the dry air can travel, thus by-passing the foliage, which otherwise is liable to get scorched.

A bowl of water in front of a gas or electric fire contributes to everybody's health and comfort, and any other little trick that helps to keep up humidity will be more than well rewarded.

We cannot be expected to damp down our rooms like a greenhouse, but remember that humidity is more important to a tropical plant than a high temperature, gas dries the atmosphere fast and a plant on the mantelpiece with a coal fire merrily burning below is condemned to death.

There are the few, of course, who survive and even enjoy dry conditions such as the aspidistra, *sansevieria* and *chlorophytum*.

## Syringing

A refresher from a syringe is an excellent reviver for tired foliage. It can be done outdoors on a warm day without any detrimental effect upon curtains and covers, but splashing of walls and furniture can be avoided by protecting them with a polythene sheet.

Gardeners who do not possess a syringe can make do by swishing with an old hair or clothes brush dipped in water or insecticide.

## Misting

This is carried out with a fine-nozzled syringe, or perhaps a giant scent or hairdresser's spray.

## Steaming

Advantage should be taken of the steaming kettle in the kitchen. It is the close, damp atmosphere of the cottage and steam from the wash-tub, stock-pot and kettle that enabled the veterans to bloom their geraniums. The cottager cultivated that difficult customer the maidenhair fern, long before the Scandinavians even thought about their foliage plants.

## Steam Bath

The moisture-loving plant, such as the cyclamen or *saintpaulia*, revels in this. The pot should be set in a small bowl; this bowl is now placed in a larger container and the latter filled with steaming water. The pot in the interior of the smaller bowl must be kept dry on its island and the plant left to delight in the vapour. This treatment may even resuscitate the distressed cyclamen that was reduced to a huddle of limp leaves shortly after its arrival from the florist. It may also breathe new life into the lovely azalea that became a sudden scarecrow with a heap of dried leaves at its miserable feet.

There is nothing to prevent the gardener taking his cyclamen and others into the bathroom while he bathes and leaving them there for the night. I shall always remember the begonias and *saintpaulias* in my American bathroom, patterned here and there with an occasional Rex (begonia). A great improvement in decor on the back-brush and other bathroom sundries.

## Pebbles and Gravel

A single plant may be stood on pebbles in a saucer, or a group of plants can be placed on a pebble and gravel tray: the pebbles and gravel should be kept constantly moist.

Warning: pots must not be allowed to stand in water, or root-rot will quickly develop.

## Sand Box

A sand box filled with 2—3 inches of wet sand is suitable for the plant dependent on humidity. Steaming water may be added to the sand to keep it moist.

## Moss and Peat

A pot may be dropped into a larger pot and the space between the pots packed with sphagnum moss or granulated peat, *both of which must be well soaked beforehand* and afterwards kept moist. A zinc-lined plant box, holding half a dozen plants or more, can be interpacked in this way and makes an ideal container. Or simpler still, the single plant may be top-dressed with sphagnum and the moss kept nicely damp; packed in a bowl of moist peat, it usually flourishes.

It will be found that leaves exude their moisture, so that the more plants there are in the room the more humid the atmosphere will be and the better for the plant community.

Summing up, aim at a steady temperature, good light and plenty of humidity. These are the three basic and essential home comforts.

◄ ASPIDISTRA.

► ANTHURIUM SCHERZERIANUM — *this plant needs humidity and warmth.*

▼ MONSTERA BORSIGIANA — *this plant requires an even heat and humidity.*

# SOIL AND CONTAINERS

A good soil compost is all-important; after all, a plant will only get out of the soil what we put into it.

House plants need very special fare; being unable to search for nourishment themselves, they are entirely at our mercy.

The countryman can steal a shovelful of 'good stuff' from the vegetable garden or lift a sod in the cow field or fill his flower-pot with treasured top spit from just below the turf. He can usually get as much leafmould as he wants from under the oak trees in the wood, line his basket with peat moss and obtain coarse river or bank sand. Sea sand and yellow builder's sand are generally injurious to plants, besides being too fine and liable to be washed away.

Well-chosen country fare is highly nourishing. It has one drawback only, it is likely to be bug-ridden. The leafmould in particular is apt to harbour pests and diseases and is a happy breeding ground.

It is easy enough to remove the worms; they should be thrown out, because they are capable of disturbing the crocks and upsetting the drainage system. But for the smaller fry and safety, sterilization is essential.

There are a number of ways of sterilizing, but the simplest method is to treat the soil like a suet dumpling by wrapping it in a cloth and steaming it for half an hour. Those who do not sterilize soil run a dangerous risk of disease and parasites.

Ordinary garden soil is rarely rich enough to sustain the confined plant and must be enriched. It can be improved in the following manner.

To 2 parts of garden soil add:

*1 part leafmould, or peat*
*1 part sharp sand*

*3 oz. of John Innes Base Fertilizer*

Beware of clay: it is helpful in retaining moisture but on the stiff side for pot work.

The town gardener is often bewildered by the many compost recipes. He may be told to provide as many as half a dozen ingredients to a mixture when all he needs is one pot-full. John Innes Potting Compost (or J. I. P. as it is known) is an answer, being suitable for most house plants. It can be bought in small quantities from the sundries man or florist, and suits the majority of indoor plants. It is ideal food for the young and moderate grower with a moderate appetite. This is the formula of the J.I.P. No. 1

*7 parts medium loam by loose bulk*
*3 parts moist horticultural peat by*
*    loose bulk*
*2 parts coarse sand by loose bulk*
*4 ounces John Innes Base Fertilizer*
*    and*
*¾ ounce ground chalk per bushel*

No. 2 Compost is a richer mixture for the faster growing and the hearty that like it rich. No. 3 Compost is for those that can take it richer still.

The J.I.P. No. 1 was originally prepared for conservatory plants. The house plant, in a drier atmosphere, benefits by an addition of granulated peat (1 part to every 2—3 of compost, depending upon the plant in question). It is important to soak and squeeze out the peat before using it, otherwise it will take all the moisture from the compost.

It is impossible to pot properly if the compost is too sticky or too crumbly, too wet or too dry. Like a pudding mixture, the compost has to be of the right

▲ *The arrangement on the right consists of:* GYNURA
SARMENTOSA, HEDERA CANARIENSIS, CROTON, RHOICIS-
SUS RHOIMBOIDEA, CRYPTANTHUS FOSTERIANUS, TRADE-
SCANTIA TRICOLOUR *and* CRYPHANTHUS TRICOLOUR.
*On the left of the picture is an arrangement of* HEDERA
ADAM *and* BEGONIA REX.

▲ *The indoor gardener should avoid keeping his plants in gloomy corners. Darkness will elongate and distort the foliage and bloom. The tall plant at the back is a* SANSEVIERIA TRIFASCIATA LAUSENTII; *the trailing plant in the front a* HEDERA, *behind which is a* SAINT-PAULIA.

▼ *Two trailing plants —* HEDERA ADAM *and* SAINT-PAULIA CAVALIER.

▶ *A group of indoor plants showing how the height of plants must be taken into consideration. Avoid having too many plants of similar height in a trough as this is seldom effective. A* FICUS LYRATA *and* HEDERA GLACIER *are shown at the back with a* HEDERA CHICAGO *to the left and a* BEGONIA REX *to the right. The plant towards the bottom of the picture is a* CYCLAMEN SILVER LEAF.

▼ *The plant on the left of the picture is a* SAINTPAULIA, *which must have light and will not bloom generously in a sunless north window. The arrangement on the right includes* HIBISCUS, HEDERA CHICAGO VARIAGATA, PEPEROMIA MAGNOLIAEFOLIA *and* PODOCARPUS SINUATUS.

▼ *The tall plant in the top left hand corner is a* PHILO-DENDRON SCANDENS. *In the top right hand corner is a selection of* CROTONS. *On the table is a* CYCLAMEN SILVER LEAF. *The arrangement in the front of the picture includes,* FICUS TRICOLOUR, DRACAENA, SCINDAPSUS MARBLE QUEEN, PEPEROMIA MAGNOLIAEFOLIA, APHELANDRA, MARANTA, HEDERA GREEN RIPPLE *and* CITRUS MITIS.

▶ ROMAN HYACINTH

consistency, and here good cooks should come off best. The gardener should be able to mould his mixture into a dumpling or ball which should crumble under its own weight and yet not cling, much less stick, to his fingers. A pinch of compost pressed between finger and thumb should smear and not crumble.

Cacti, succulents and desert dwellers enjoy an open soil and a fast runaway. A good all-round potting mixture consists of 3 parts loam, 2 parts sharp river sand, 1 part thoroughly decomposed leafmould, 2 parts broken brick (about 1—¼ inch) and ½ part of broken old mortar rubble. The addition of a little charcoal will help to keep the soil sweet. But of course there are plants with individual tastes that have to be studied, such as the *Epiphyllum* that can't stand lime.

## Summing Up

A healthy plant requires a substantial amount of slowly available food, and it is good policy to give it as rich a helping as it can manage. Some plants, as indeed some people, over-eat and suffer from indigestion, while others have to be tempted with tasty morsels. The gardener should get to know his plant and the amount it can comfortably digest. If he mixes his own compost, he has an advantage in that he can omit certain of the ingredients when wishing to please a particular plant (the acid-loving require more peat than is supplied in J.I.P.). But unless he has a passion for mixing his own and if he is a beginner, be he countryman or townsman, he will be well advised to buy John Innes Compost ready-mixed. We have to thank the research institute at Bayfordbury, Hert-

fordshire, for developing a compost that is balanced to perfection.

Because of this carefully measured balance, I am no believer in the addition of too many etceteras. However, a few small lumps of charcoal will keep the soil sweet while cloaking any disturbing smell.

How long will John Innes satisfy your plant? Two years or more. It gives up its nutriment slowly throughout this period. So long as your plant looks happy and the foliage neither discolours nor prematurely falls all is well. Let it remain so.

## Soil-less Culture

Plants can be grown in a sterile medium if they are fed with a nutrient solution. Vermiculite is ideal in retaining both air and moisture. It is disease free, promotes the growth of seedlings with complete absence of damping off and creates a healthy root system. The particles of this golden-looking sand are so light that it is possible to transplant without damaging the root hairs.

The gardener who has difficulty in obtaining soil may care to experiment with a mixture of vermiculite and sand. He will need a watertight container and a layer of drainage material covered by glass wool should be placed at the bottom.

The method reduces the need for both watering and re-potting as the soil does not sour. It is particularly helpful in growing the African Violet (see page 115).

Gardeners on the Continent (particularly in Germany) like the idea of feeding their plants by solution; we in this country have not yet overcome an old fashioned prejudice and most of us keep to soil.

## Containers and Pot Holders

The battle between the clay and glazed pot still rages in the States. Those who stand for 'the clay' enjoy its unbeatable porous quality and reasonable price; those in favour of 'the glazed' benefit by the moisture retained in the pudding and the economy of their labour with the can. The nurseryman appreciates the fact that they are almost indestructible.

The glazed pot can be had in all shapes, colours and sizes; it is a pity when its colour and design compete with the plant for attention, but this is a matter of taste or pocket.

Providing the pot has a drainage hole, a veritable safety valve, the choice is of little importance.

There are also pot-hiders in great variety into

Left and below. Attractive and unusual plant containers.

Below left. GOLDEN HELXINE ('mind your own business') in a blue and white wedgwood bowl.

Below right. GERANIUM STAND.

which a terracotta pot can be slipped. These, without drainage holes certainly spare the polished table, but there is the danger of forgetting to empty the accumulated drip. A plant may stand with its feet in water, suffering untold agonies, yet the gardener may notice nothing amiss until serious damage is done.

If so wished, clay pots can be painted with flat oil paint; white or green are becoming colours. The pots must be painted before planting is done, and the gardener should remember that when treated in this way they will become less porous and require less attention from the can.

Soup tureens and coppers are used as plant furniture with good effect, but, alas, they have no runaways. Beyond these there a host of whimsy containers, some of which make me sigh for the common pot.

With the exception of our new schools and larger buildings, the modern architect has not yet given us the compromised built-in garden trough, so we have to make do with a metal trough or a table trolley on wheels. The table trolley is handy; it can be moved away from the window on a cold night and placed out of range of the midday summer's sun. I like the *jardinière*, too, and the movable screen with hooks to which pots can be fastened. These can be amusingly patterned with wire, wood, basket work, split bamboo, raffia or plastic (light and unbreakable) containers.

A baby's bath is sometimes used for mass planting, while biscuit barrels come in for the more spectacular subjects.

A three or four-tier saucepan stand, attractively painted, makes a satisfactory holder for a small number of plants, while a trellis between the kitchen and dining-room, or framing the window, gives the climber welcome assistance and always wins admiration.

As a basket fan I recommend the new osier and cane shapes that are readily available and, in particular, the attractive bird-cage and the hock bottle designs.

Drip catchers have to be considered; they are generally sold with the fancy pot. If not, painted tin lids will be found efficient, but the odd saucer, so easy to wash, has always been my choice.

If you keep your plant in its pot, you will be able to give it individual attention and watering, and it is easy to camouflage a group effect with moss. Need I add that a plant should never be removed from its pot and rammed into a smaller container? This is one of the deadly sins in gardening.

**Plant Arrangements**

The grouping of his plants is largely the gardener's affair and will much depend upon his purse and taste; some people, of course, prefer the single specimen. But the gardener who proposes to group his plants in a single container, whether it be in tiers, stands, troughs or tubs, must be particular to put those that have the same cultural needs together. The *sansevieria*, cactus and succulents are good company; but should he also introduce *Ficus pumilla*, Umbrella Plant and *selaginella*, all moisture-lovers, he will find it impossible to please them all. This applies to peat and

◀ KLANCHOE — *succulent plants with vivid clusters of blooms.*

▼ VARIEGATED ASPIDISTRA.

lime fans; never will these two meet, so find plants that have the same likes and dislikes before uniting them.

Height is an important point; too many plants of similar height in a trough are seldom effective.

The gardener should study the colour of the foliage, its texture and shape and the character of his plants. He will find the *tradescantia* willing and helpful in filling uninteresting corners; it also breaks hard edges and dull lines. The *philodendron* will readily disguise the poorness and shortcomings of a neighbour, and in the larger arrangements, two or three of any kind will give a bold, rich and lush effect.

So far as house plants go I have none of the priggery of the purist, and see nothing wrong in introducing a bright annual from the garden in the summer or autumn or a glamorous stove plant from the hot-house in the winter. I like a splash of colour, so difficult to find in a house plant, among the greenery.

So, if you have the chance, add a gloxinia, azalea, cyclamen or cineraria to your winter design. Or in the autumn lift a pansy, antirrhinum, geranium or stock from the garden border and plant it in your trough. If the annuals have already flowered they are valueless; a second performance is out of the question. But there are usually a few late annual seedlings — slowcoaches that have buds on them which can be rescued from the frost. This is to everybody's advantage. Maybe you can dig up a primrose in the wood stometime in February; if you bring it indoors, keep it cool and watered from the bottom — it may flower a few weeks earlier than is its habit. It will look charming tucked in with the small foliage.

Now each to his taste! You may care to introduce your bronzes, china or strange and unrelated subjects into your house plant composition. The indoor gardener, unlike the flower decorator, has no prescribed and tiresome 'focal point' or rules to follow. But please retain a sense of proportion; too many plants in a room are an error and a bore.

# WATERING

"How often should I water my house plant?" asks the beginner. Alas, there is no clear-cut answer.

During a normal summer, a growing plant will certainly require a drink once or twice a week. But if the sun is hot and the plant shows signs of flagging, it may well need water every day. Only you can decide when and how much, so the beginner has to learn the art of using the watering-can with discretion. Skill is achieved with experience, by studying the plants day by day and getting to know them.

Give your plant water when it is thirsty and do not follow a once or twice a week routine; the 'little and often' method of 'dribs and drabs' is a bad one. The speed with which a plant will dry out depends on many things, all of which you will have to take into consideration.

1. Some plants require more water than others. The *sansevieria*, a desert Snake Plant, should be watered sparingly; the *impatiens*, or Patient Lucy, will lap up right through the summer, growing daily before your eyes and flowering freely. Cacti and succulents need little moisture during the winter. No two plants drink alike.

2. Weather, humidity and temperature play an important part. Plants in a hot, dry atmosphere or exposed to continual sunshine require constant attention with the watering-can.

3. Plants in small pots need more water than those in large pots. Newly potted plants should be watered cautiously until they have settled down.

4. A thick soil that holds the water will dry out more slowly than one with a high sand content.

5. Much will depend upon the pot; the ordinary porous pot loses more moisture by evaporation through its sides than a glazed container.

6. The drainage system must be constantly checked. If the pot is efficiently crocked there will be an easy run-away. If the drainage is faulty the water will be held in the pot. An otherwise friendly worm may well be responsible for the hold-up and must be evicted.

7. Lastly, much will depend on the health of your plant and whether it is growing or dormant. When a plant is active, generally in the summer, it will need more water than during the resting period. A sick plant should be given little to drink but enough to prevent it drying out altogether.

Watering is best done in the morning with rain water at room temperature. Rain water leaves no disfiguring white spots or deposits on the foliage and is softer than tap water. Very cold water is injurious to sensitive roots. In the winter the gardener can stand a can of tap water in a warm room to take the chill off. It is better that the temperature of the drink should be a little warmer than the room.

In cold weather, water your plants early in the day so that the water is absorbed before the temperature falls in the evening. Plants do not enjoy being cold and wet any more than we do.

Plants which are potted to the brim with soil should be dipped in a bucket of water. Let the pot stay with half its depth in the bucket until the water seeps through the surface soil, and the bubbles cease to rise.

▶ A SELECTION OF CACTI — *they need very little water during the winter.*

*Above.* HIPPEASTRUM — *until the flower buds appear apply water sparingly.*

*Top.* ZYGOCACTUS TRUNCACTUS — *once this plant has flowered it should be kept on the dry side.*

Now two stern don'ts: *don't* let your plant stand in a saucer of water. Empty saucers soon after watering: there are few plants that enjoy their toes in the wet. They are not aquatics. *Don't* let your pot get water-logged if you can help it; more plants die from too much water than from too little. A pot without a drainage hole is a menace; a drink too many and flooding is inevitable. If this happens the only hope is to turn the pot upside down and let the surplus water drain away. Quite a ticklish job to do without damaging the plant.

When first watered, a thirsty plant may quickly soak up the given measure and may immediately be filled up a second time.

Gauging the amount of moisture in the soil is important, because it will help you in judging how much water the plant can comfortably take. You should first study the plant and the soil. Soil that has become light in colour is usually dry. Caked soil is sometimes difficult to judge: you may scrape the soil to the depth of half an inch (without disturbing the roots) to get a clearer picture of the situation — for appearances can be most deceiving. Soil may look dry on the surface but be sodden below, or equally bone dry beneath and damp on top — often the consequence of 'drib and drab' drinks.

Now confirm your opinion by getting the feel and the weight of the pot. A light pot means a dry pot. Make a habit of lifting and testing its weight before and after watering. Lastly, rap your knuckles outside the pot; you will soon get to know the hollow ring of a dry plant and the dull, sullen note that indicates moisture.

## Summing Up

It can now be seen that the problems are too numerous and varied for the gardener to water automatically on any said day. He must be guided not by the calendar but by the plants themselves. Most plants rest from October until April and need little water during this period. But water the plant that flags and none must be allowed to go desert dry.

## Wick Watering

By this method water is taken from a small reservoir (maybe the butter dish) through a wick and passed on to the soil and plant roots.

The wick must be long enough to allow it to reach comfortably from the water container to the pot where it enters the drainage hole and folds over inside

the bottom of the pot. A little extra length must be allowed so that the wick can be teased out and tufted at both ends. This is best installed at potting-up time.

Certain saintpaulia growers swear by this 'self-watering' or watering by capillarity. They have their own method of supporting a plant over the reservoir; perhaps a metal plate on which the plant is stood when the whole affair is rested on a kitchen baking pan holding the water.

Wick watering is a tip for summer weekends and brief holidays when the gardener is off duty. It is by no means a foolproof business and should never be practised on the cactus, succulents, *sansevieria* and those that like it dry.

Porous clay cones, pointed affairs that can be filled with water, are sometimes used on the Continent for holiday watering: however, I have not seen these cones on the market in this country.

*Top left. Watering is best done in the morning with rain water at room temperature.*

*Top right.* CHRYSANTHEMUM — *when plants become very dry stand them in a bowl of water.*

*Above.* AECHMEA RHODOCYANEA — *a plant whose leaves taper to a funnel in the centre, into which water should be poured.*

# POTTING

I learnt to pot in the shed with Gilbert our gardener when I was under seven. It was he who taught that whereas the plant in the border could fend for itself, the pot plant or cutting was entirely dependent on me and its future, in every sense, very much in my hands. I felt the responsibility heavy on my shoulders. The plant had to be well planted and its first demand was a clean pot.

## Pots

The house plant usually sits in a 60 or 48 pot. The smaller the size the greater the number; the 72 is only 2½ inches in diameter and is known as a 'thumb'.

Pots should be scrubbed and well dried before use, and new ones soaked in a bucket of water for about 24 hours beforehand. Some gardeners soak pots for a couple of hours, while others will not use them unless they have been in the bucket for a week. It is amazing how much a thirsty clay pot will drink; if it isn't given its fill, it will rob the moisture from the soil.

Dirty pots often carry disease, or entertain red spiders and beasties and need hard scrubbing. Steel wool is helpful in removing obstinate encrustations. A clean pot is important, enabling the gardener to slip the root ball in and out for inspection with the minimum of disturbance.

## Crocking

A good drainage system and a well-organized run-away between crocks is vital.

The gardener should take three broken crocks and place these concave fragments, hollow side down, over the drainage hole. The crocks should be large enough to fold over the hole comfortably, and must be clean. They are often infected with disease but a 5 minutes' boil in a saucepan will sterilize them. Pieces of clay pot are preferable to broken plates for this purpose being more arched and less sharp and dangerous.

When visiting a modern house plant nursery in Denmark I did not see a single crocked pot: the most perfect porous compost was being used, so crocks were looked upon as waste of effort. However, my advice still stands — crock, and crock carefully. Few possess that lovely porous soil and the conditions that permit them to do otherwise.

## Roughage

To keep the drainage hole free and open, crocks should be covered with roughage capable of retaining moisture and at the same time preventing the compost clogging the aperture after watering.

Roughage is present in maiden top spit soil; it is the coarser part of the compost, such as the residue after sieving. Inch layers of decayed leaves, sphagnum moss (soaked and squeezed), fibrous peat, or a thick layer of turf, grass side down, will all serve to keep the drainage hole free. Crocks and roughage should fill up to a quarter of the pot.

## Compost and Plant

Now comes a thin layer of compost, which should be slightly moist without being sticky (see Soil, page 18). This should be lightly pressed down with the cushions of the fingers. Keep your thumbs out of it until it comes to firming up. If you give the pot a tap on the

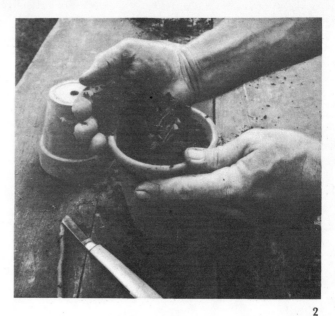

1

2

POTTING A CYCLAMEN *1. — holding the stem in one hand while the other hand is ready to dribble in the soil.*

POTTING A CYCLAMEN *2. — the soil being put around the stem.*

POTTING A CYCLAMEN *3. — working the soil down with the fingers.*

POTTING A CYCLAMEN *4. — allow about ½-inch space between the soil and the rim of the pot for watering.*

3

4

bench as you go along, it will settle the soil.

The plant should be carefully examined before it is put in. If the root ball is parched, it must be soaked before planting. This is also the moment to cut off damaged roots with the sharpest knife available. Wiry outside roots may be cut back in moderation to induce fresh growth and the fibrous roots gently spread out so that fine soil can be introduced among them. If the plant is an ugly or awkward shape, it may be lightly pruned; if pruning is delayed until after planting, the roots are liable to be jerked or loosened from their new moorings.

### Depth of Planting

Holding the stem in one hand while the other hand is ready to dribble in the soil, the depth of planting has to be decided. Naturally much will depend upon the species of plant. Tastes differ, but in time the novice will get to know the *hippeastrums* and cyclamen, which insist upon being half exposed, the ferns, who equally resent being buried, and the palm that rises up of its own accord, whatever you do. Creepers too are something of a problem; the novice should aim at burying roots only and not stems, otherwise the latter are apt to soften and decay.

The novice who is doubtful as to how deep he should plant should first study the soil mark on the stem and plant at that level. Remember that, as the soil settles, plants have a habit of sinking to a slightly lower level, so make allowance accordingly.

### Planting Firmly

Thumbs and a short potting stick of about ½-inch

in diameter are helpful for working down the soil. A broom handle, properly shaped, makes a satisfactory tamping stick.

The general rule for firmness of potting is based on the texture of the plant itself. The wiry carnation and woody fuchsia must be potted hard, while the softer tuberous begonia responds to lighter fingers.

A kind but fatherly firmness is advised. But although the compost should be firmly pressed down, the novice must avoid planting too tight and packing the soil. It is said that a rose cannot be too solidly planted. I doubt this. I have seen many a rose uncomfortably placed, drooping mournfully from what had the appearance of a macadam surround. On the other hand, a sloppy planter gets nowhere, never bringing roots and soil together. The plant that succeeds is the one given a comfortable root run. Only the large and tough require ramming.

A ½-inch space between the soil and the rim of the pot should be allowed for watering. The soil surface can now be evened with a light movement of the fingers and a last tap of the pot on the bench. Once the job is done, a generous drink can be given.

# RE-POTTING

It is much easier to tell the novice *how* to re-pot than *when* to do so. The latter question is often a problem to the veteran. Whatever the situation, it should be remembered that the smaller the pot the safer the house plant is likely to be. It will dry out quickly and a tight-fitting pot encourages flowering; the gardener should wait until the plant is pot-bound before acting.

A house plant seldom needs a larger pot every year. There are of course exceptions; the strapping young eucalyptus will want a bigger container each year and sometimes benefits by an interim move. On the other hand, an American told me her flowering cactus had remained in the same pot for a quarter of a century.

It is impossible to say how often a plant should be re-potted; it depends upon the type of plant and species, the plant's state of health and the condition of the soil.

## Best Time of Year for Re-potting

March and April are good months; this gives the plant the spring and summer to establish itself before the winter.

Plants that take a summer rest should be moved at the end of their resting period just when they wake up and begin to develop shoots either at the tips of the plant or at soil level.

To find out whether the plant is pot-bound, the gardener may 'knock' it out and inspect. The plant to be repotted should be in a dryish but not desert dry condition.

## Turning out the Pot

The left hand should be spread over the soil, the first and second fingers holding the stem firmly between them, and then the pot inverted. If the root ball is slightly moist, as it should be, tap on the rim of the pot on a hard surface and out it will slip. If it sticks, a push with a pencil through the drainage hole is a useful trick.

The plant should never be yanked out; better far to break the pot with a hammer.

Roots should be inspected at least once a year, but however sure the potter's touch, no plant approves frequent up-ending. New roots are easily recognised by their whiteness.

## Grading of Pots

If the outside of the root ball is a network of roots, re-potting is needed. It seems that the novice has a natural tendency to overpot, but this leads to water-logging, damping off and trouble. There is nothing to be gained by giving a plant more food than it can take. The pot that is a fraction larger will usually give ample space.

## The Healthy and the Young

Only a few plants stand still; the young and normal grow in size after a year or two and therefore need larger premises. It is generally easy enough to distinguish the young plant that is pressing for more elbow room and nourishment with its hungry roots forcing their way through the drainage hole. Others will have made so much foliage that they look top heavy and a little foolish in such a small pot. If they are not re-potted, they will suffer from their confinement.

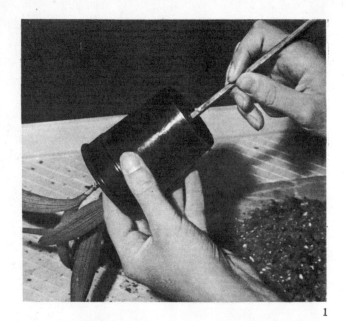

RE-POTTING *1. — push the plant out by means of a small stick or pencil through the drainage hole.*

RE-POTTING *2. — the root-ball exposed.*

RE-POTTING *3. — the plant is supported in a new pot and fresh soil added.*

RE-POTTING *4.—working the soil down the fissure between the side of the pot and the pudding.*

1

2

3
4

► RE-POTTING *5. — when the plant has been re-potted give it a drink, but do not water again until the soil is almost dry.*

5

## The Sick Plant

This is the problem child! It is a tricky and uphill business nursing a sick plant in a house or flat.

If the soil looks sour and lifeless (the plant not having had the courage to absorb the moisture given), then maybe something has to be done, but the operation involves risk and often ends in failure. The move may hasten death.

The sick and the aged on the slippery slope will have sparse roots lacking in vitality. They should be given a simple diet, a light compost easy to digest without manure or fertilizer. For those that have shrunk in size, a smaller pot should be provided.

To the novice who is undecided as to whether to move the invalid, my advice is this: if the drainage system is in order and the water running freely through the pot, content yourself with top dressing (see opposite). I have seldom regretted leaving the ailing in peace.

## Re-potting

Having turned out the pot, cut back unhealthy roots. Carefully tease away the crocks and exhausted soil from the pudding. This is also the moment to divide plants (see p. 51) or to wean offsets from the parent (see p. 51). Now go forward as for potting crocks first, roughage next and so on (see page 32). Then holding the plant in a central position and to its best advantage, fill the margin between the pot and the root ball with the compost. The thin potting stick will come in handy, helping to work the soil down the narrow fissure between the side of the pot and the pudding.

Give the plant a drink and do not water again until the soil is almost dry.

## Top Dressing

This is a lesser and often an alternative operation to re-potting, undertaken when the plant requires more food but has enough foot room. It consists in scraping away the top 1—3 inches of soil from the pot, taking every care not to injure the roots. Some gardeners flush the exhausted soil away under the tap, but this often proves a messy business.

The pot or tub must now be replenished with J.I.P. No. 2 or any good soil with a fertilizer or manure content. ½ teaspoonful of bone meal is excellent (not for the azalea or heaths) and sand or peat can be added if it is desired to lighten the soil.

## Top dressing is suitable for:

● The large plant in a heavy tub or container.
● The temperamental plant that resents being moved (the *hippeastrum* prefers to remain undisturbed even if it means breaking the pot with its roots).
● The plant that is growing freely but is not yet pot-bound.
● The plant where a hard crust has formed on the top of the soil, or when the soil is sour. The novice cannot be expected to detect sourness, but he should top dress when the soil has ceased to be crumbly and healthy looking.

Tubs and pots should be top dressed every 9 or 12 months, either while the plant is resting or on its awaking.

There is usually a generous response to this freshening attention.

# GENERAL CARE

## Cleaning and Grooming

It is important to keep up appearances, and the gardener should not grudge time taken in seeing that his plants are clean; indeed, cleanliness means as much to a plant as to a human being.

Sponging of leaves with warm water, or if necessary a little soap and water, removes the grime which so quickly collects on the occupants of the window-sill. If you live near a railway station or in a factory area, the deposit can become a danger to health for, beyond looking shocking, the plant's breathing apparatus gets blocked. A plant may need grooming once a fortnight or once a year; much will depend on where you live. The gardener should not groom by the calendar but only when necessary.

The fuzzy, downy and hairy-leaved such as the African Violet should never be washed but dusted down with a soft brush; dirt should be gently stroked away in the same manner from cacti and succulents.

Here is the best way of cleaning your plant. A syringe or spray should be followed by a wipe with a soft cotton rag or sponge that has been dipped in warm water and wrung dry. If you put a supporting hand under the leaf, you will save any wear and tear.

Now comes a highly debatable point. Should the leaves be cleaned with warm water, soft soap and water, milk, skimmed milk, brown ale, white oil emulsion, furniture polish or what have you? My choice is warm water and a little soft soap when necessary. Oil is bound to clog a little and will certainly attract further dust. Of the rest I prefer skimmed milk as being the least likely to block pores. The gardener must keep the plant in the shade until

it is dry. A bead of moisture caught by the sun will scorch a leaf.

Nurserymen use Volck, a spraying oil and their plants are seen groomed to perfection at Chelsea and Southport.

Oil has the advantage of acting as a pesticide against red spider — making it impossible for the latter to move about and feed. A weak mixture is advised (not more than 1 dessertspoonful to 1 gallon) otherwise leaves may suffer and their appearance become unattractively oily.

We all like to see glistening foliage, be it natural sheen and lustre or artificial shine and gloss, but spit and polish can be overdone at the expense of the plant. The *philodendron* can be made to shine like a boot, but some plants suffer from too much valeting.

## Feeding and Fertilizers

A healthy plant bought from a nursery or shop should be self-supporting for 3 months. If the basic mixture in which it is planted possesses the right mineral salts and the plant is not pot-bound, the soil will need a minimum of care for some time.

Supplementary feeding can be dangerous so please heed this warning. To feed a sick or waterlogged plant merely accentuates trouble. However, the pot-bound and the rapid grower, especially those whose leaves are getting smaller while their growth is losing vigour, need a pick-me-up.

The gardener must see that the soil is nicely moist before feeding and should water after the application. This is a precaution against burning sensitive rootlets.

Next the stimulant has to be decided upon. Weak

▼ COBAEA SCANDENS — *a plant with mauve, bell-shaped flowers and oval leaves.*

◀ *An arrangement of indoor plants showing* CROTON, PHILODENDRON BURGUNDY, HEDERA CHICAGO VARIE-GATA *and* PEPEROMIA MAGNOLIAEFOLIA.

manure is of course the thing; 1 cup of dried cow manure, bagged and suspended in a gallon of water for 4 weeks, will possess qualities beyond compare. The liquid should be diluted if necessary to the colour described as weak tea, straw or pale amber. But liquid cow or sheep manure is seldom available in a London flat and the brew has an odour not acceptable to most of us.

Plantoids, plant tablets, Clay's Fertilizer, bone meal and powders are useful stimulants and handy; tablets should be pushed down at the side of the pot away from the plant. But these products cannot possibly give such an even performance as a liquid, and for this reason I recommend John Innes Feed (J.I.L.) Luxigrow, or Bio.

The complete fertilizer suits most plants. It contains nitrogen, phosphorus and potash. Roughly speaking, nitrogen promotes foliage and growth and good green colouring; phosphates assist in the formation of flowers, fruits, seeds and roots, and potash helps plants to resist disease while strengthening growth. It balances the nitrogen by stiffening stems and soft growth. Thus it will be clear that a flowering plant that runs to foliage and fails to bloom should not be given a fertilizer with a high nitrogen content.

The novice will get to know the look of the yellow, hungry plant. A plant such as *Cobaea scandens*, that climbs by the yard, may need as many as three feeds during its short life, and flowering plants usually have a big appetite. He will before long recognize the lank, pale plant that has been overfed with fertilizer and is suffering from indigestion and sappy growth.

To the beginner I offer the following advice.

## Don't feed:

● A sick plant, or you will place its life in peril.
● The new arrival, until it has become acclimatized to your home and you.
● The newly potted; give the plant at least three months to settle down.
● The plant that is resting; most plants rest in the winter from September to April. Feeding should begin when the plant wakes up and starts to grow and should go on through spring and summer.
● A dry plant.
● The plant that is not pot-bound and is in flourishing form. Leave well alone.
● The plant that is about to flower, once its buds have coloured. (This applies more to some plants than others, and to the Christmas Cactus in particular.)

These are golden rules to which I add two last warnings. Overfeeding is a temptation; follow the manufacturer's instructions on the fertilizer packet or you will be in trouble. Give a little less rather than a little more, and no — repeat no — double doses. This point has to be stressed, as strangely even the meanest of men become wildly generous with the fertilizer tin.

At all cost avoid fresh manure. Enthusiastic gardeners seen in the street with searching eye and empty shovel are on the wrong track. Manure must be thoroughly well decayed, which is a matter of long months before it can be used, otherwise it tends to burn plant roots.

Try to understand your plants. Some, among them many of the *Bromeliads*, will appreciate feeding less than others.

## Staking

Stakes should be as inconspicuous as possible, and inserted close to the stem without interfering with plant roots. The supports should be slightly shorter than the stem or shoots. The knot of the string or base tie must be made against the stake and not next to the stem or plant, with allowance for growth and swelling. The ties should be inspected throughout the growing season.

On no account must a plant be bunched up or surrounded by a scaffolding of sticks; shoots should be spread out so that the plant is well balanced. Brushwood stakes attract less notice than canes. Natural cut hazel supports are the best of all for aerial roots. Staking is a knack in which the novice seldom excels; the stakes are for the plant's comfort and support and

41

should not take the form of a vice. Start staking early and thus avoid damaging plant roots.

Finger the foliage as little as possible while doing this work. Leaves mark extremely easily and no plant welcomes the human hand.

## Pruning

This is a controversial subject, but of no great concern to the house plant gardener. Stragglers like the *tradescantia* must be firmly handled but the majority of house plants are neat and tidy.

The gardener pinches (a finger-and-thumb operation) to induce the formation of side shoots and bushiness and perhaps to enable the *philodendron* to turn the corner from curtain to pelmet. He prunes the gawky-shaped plant, hoping it will break out from the base and so gain a smarter appearance.

Pruning and pinching should be performed just above a leaf which has a bud pointing in the direction the gardener wishes the plant to travel. If a branch is to be removed it is better to cut close to the junction of the parent branch or trunk; stubs are ugly and ruin a plant's line and character. The novice should concentrate on cutting out dead wood and encouraging new growth from the base of the plant. He should keep his secateurs sharp and master the art of handling a knife, while using both with discretion.

I found the Danish house plants were apt to be out of control: they rambled and romped and much of their distinction was lost in a tangled jungle.

Pruning is usually best done after flowering and towards the end of the resting period (before the plant begins to grow actively). Constant snipping is un-

▶ *Don't feed a plant which has been newly potted — it will need at least 3 months to settle down.*

▼ COBAEA SCANDENS — *a plant that climbs by the yard which may need as many as 3 feeds during its life.*

forgivable. The geranium and fuchsia and others that benefit by pruning and those that require special treatment are dealt with under their own headings.

Although pruning should result in bushy and more vigorous growth a temporary check may be expected. So go steady with the watering can.

### The Resting Period

When active growth gradually stops, after flowering or fruiting or at certain times of the year, the plant is said to be resting (this does not mean that its roots are at a standstill).

Many plants, including the cacti and succulents, take their rest in the winter; others, among them bulbs and cyclamen, lie dormant in the summer. All these plants need and depend upon repose if they are expected to give a wholehearted performance the following year.

Growth cycles differ, but if you watch your plant closely you will learn to sense its desire to take a nap. Then gradually cut down the water supply and keep the plant cool, avoiding abrupt changes of night temperatures.

Some resting periods are more pronounced than others. I have seen a Christmas Cactus spurred into activity by heavy watering and heat when it should have been allowed to mark time. It repaid the gardener by refusing to flower the following year. There are plants that will not be dragooned; they will take their siesta at their chosen time whatever the gardener may do.

Although the static plant requires little to drink, it must not be allowed to dry out completely and

◀ CACTI — *the dirt should be gently stoked away from the leaves with a soft brush.*

▼ FUCHSIA — *this plant will benefit from a spell in the garden.*

wilting or withering must be avoided. Manures in any form must be withheld altogether until the plant is well on the move again.

So please do not stimulate, turn out, move, sponge or even dust the sleeping plant. Give it perfect peace and in its own good time it will burst forth.

### Fresh Air

House plants are fresh-air lovers and the majority enjoy a blow on the window-sill on a warm spring, summer or autumn day. Fresh air hardens a plant ready for the winter; to over-cosset a plant makes it delicate.

Now two evils that bedevil the indoor plant, draught and poisonous fumes, particularly those of gas, coke and anthracite.

### Draught

Plants have a horror of draught; it is a lightning killer; and a badly fitting window or a slamming door will affect the tough as well as the sensitive. A *cineraria* placed on a table between an open window and door on a blowy day will collapse in no time.

### Fumes

It seems that plants and flowers can detect a leaking gas-pipe quicker than the gardener. I have known a carnation pucker up its petals when the fumes have escaped the notice of the householder. Finally the flower has died. The tomato plant is another with a keen sense of smell.

There are a number of plants that stand up to gas fumes better than others; they are those with strong constitutions and leathery leaves, such as the sanseviera and ivy. Cacti and succulents will also put up with small doses.

Unburnt fumes are the most dangerous; they cause a discoloration of foliage and, if constant, are apt to kill. In towns there is smog for which as yet there is no remedy.

### Flowering Failure

It is sometimes difficult to discover why a certain plant that looks in perfectly good health stubbornly refuses to bloom.

The gardener should run through a short check-up, always bearing in mind his plant's particular likes and dislikes:

Soil?
Temperature?

Humidity?

Light?

Ventilation?

Flowering failure happens on occasion. Why? I've known a plant beat a brains trust of horticulturists on this very subject, the reason for flower failure remaining a mystery.

However, it is clear that a plant that flowers profusely year by year is healthy.

## A Holiday in the Garden

There is a great advantage in being able to give certain plants such as the fuchsia or begonia a summer outing in the garden. Not only does the fresh air, sun, rain and dew help them to recuperate from the strain of indoor life but enables them to store up vitality.

It is better to leave the plants in their pots, otherwise there may be difficulty in returning them to confinement at the end of the holiday. Plunge the pot into the ground right up to the rim. If buried deeper,

▼ CHRISTMAS CACTUS — *this plant is dormant during the winter, so cut down the water supply and keep the plant cool.*

plants are inclined to send out top roots that will have to be cut away when they are lifted. A layer of cinders for the pots to stand upon prevents roots escaping into the earth.

A semi-shady spot should be found for the house plants; they are not accustomed to the elements. When the end of summer comes and before indoor heating is begun, pots should be taken up, cleaned, top dressed with good compost to which ½ teaspoonful of fertilizer may be added, and then returned to their positions.

A spell in the garden is an aid to beauty.

### Your Holiday

If you go away in the winter and there is to be no heating in your absence, move the plants away from the window and leave them slightly moist.

If you go in the summer, pack them round in damp moss or peat. Some gardeners will prefer to wick water (see page 30).

▼ SPARMANNIA AFRICANA — *the hairy leaves of this plant should be dusted down with a soft brush.*

# PROPAGATION

Taking cuttings is the simplest way of increasing 'true' or identical stock. Some plants, such as the geranium Paul Crampel, if left to seed produce most unworthy offspring.

## Rooting Mediums
There are four to choose from:
1. A pot three-quarters full with sterilized soil (J.I.S.), topped with 1-inch layer of sharp white sand (from the nurseryman).
2. A half-and-half mixture of sand and peat moss.
3. A horticultural form of vermiculite preferably mixed with sharp sand (delightfully clean to handle).
4. Water (for certain plants only).

The novice should note that cuttings rooted in the last three mediums must be moved on into nourishing soil as soon as they have grown a few strong roots.

## Propagating Case
A close steady atmosphere makes strikings surer and faster.

The modern house-plant man may possess an electrically heated propagator or a professionally heated fish tank, the handyman will fit up a battery jar, while others like myself make do with an inverted jam jar. Alternatively I slip a 5-inch pot into a larger pot and then cover it with a sheet of glass.

A home-made propagating box with 4 glass sides rising 6-inches above the box, held together with transparent tape and finished with a removable glass cover (larger than the box) can be very efficient. It should be lined with sphagnum moss, filled with sand or vermiculite, which can be kept damp by resting the box for a short time in a tray of warm water.

Cuttings should be kept close with the lid on for about two weeks, the glass being removed once a day and wiped. Once the cuttings perk up they should be admitted to the air by gradual stages and the lid taken away within three weeks.

If a cutting requires heat in order to strike, the box may be placed close by a radiator (helped by the addition of hormone powder), but at no time should the temperature rise above 75°F.

## Stem Cutting
This is the softwood, shoot, and most usual form of house plant cutting. It will vary between 4—8 inches in length (according to species); it should be taken below a leaf joint or node and the cut made upwards with a sharp knife or razor. Go lightly with your thumb; bruised tissue is likely to decay.

Experienced gardeners can tell at a glance the shoot that will make a virile plant. It must not be too hard or too sappy; it must possess neither buds nor flowers, and above all not straggle. The brittle cutting of the current year's growth that snaps rather than breaks is the one that succeeds. The selection of the suitable shoot is seldom stressed but it is an important part of the business and the parent plant should be well watered before the cutting is taken.

When the shoot is severed, the lower leaves should be trimmed away, leaving about one-third of its length bare. If using a pot, it should be scrubbed and dry. Cuttings will tuck up an inch apart next to the rim of the pot where it is warm; if pushed into the parent pot, moving them becomes a disturbing affair.

1

AIR LAYERING *1 — a notch is cut through the stem at the
point where you wish the roots to form.*

2

AIR LAYERING *2 — the notch surrounded with moss.*

AIR LAYERING *3 — binding the moss with polythene.*

3

AIR LAYERING *4 — securing the polythene with cellophane
tape.*

4

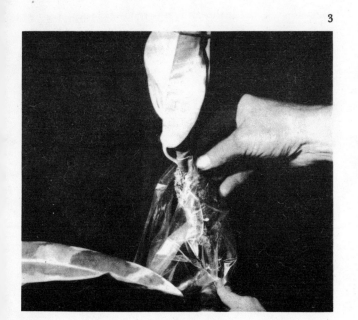

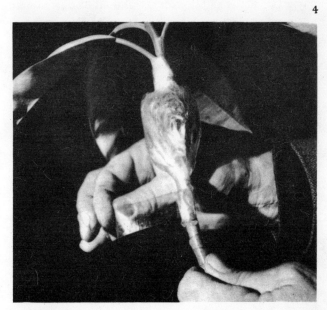

1

A grove of cuttings or seedlings generally do better than a single as they seem to enjoy company.

Before planting, water well then, making a hole with a thin stick or pencil, let the sand trickle down the channel to form a dry cushion and insert the cutting firmly. If the cutting flags, water it.

The first three weeks may be a matter of life and death. Protection must be given from the strong sun and frost, and the sand kept constantly damp. In a short time the unrooted will damp off while the survivors perk up. These, when actively growing, may be moved to private pots.

Soft-tissued plants, among them geraniums and succulents, benefit if the cuttings are allowed to lie quiet for a few hours before planting so that the cut surface dries and the callus starts forming. Fleshy cuttings (cactus and succulents) should be dusted with charcoal to prevent bleeding. Stem cuttings are best taken in the spring or autumn.

### Heel Cuttings

A heel cutting is generally taken from a woody plant; it includes some of the old and half-ripened wood. It seldom looks back.

### Leaf Cuttings

This is an excellent way of propagating the begonia (see page 100) and saintpaulia (see page 115). Succulents will also grow from a single leaf. Cuttings are best taken in the summer or the growing season.

### Root Cuttings

A root cutting taken at potting time should be laid horizontally, 1-inch below the soil (of a high sand content), care being taken to plant the right way up.

### Layering

Many plants send out runners that make easy rooted cuttings; these stems have plantlets at their tips that can be detached and soon form independent plants.

This is the principle of layering: make a slanting incision, half-way through a low pliable stem; stripping it of leaves, bend and secure it with a peg or hairpin into a mound or top dressing of leafmould and sand. The cut should be kept open and hormone powder sprinkled into the incision to hasten root formation. When the callus has formed, roots will appear and, now self-supporting, the layer may be weaned from its parent. This operation takes about 5 weeks and success will depend on secure pegging. The honey-suckle provides most accommodating side shoots for learners to practise upon.

### Air Layering

A layer can be had by this method from a shoot of the parent, from such plants as the India-rubber, large philo or *monstera*. Roots are struck on the stem trunk by cutting a notch $\frac{1}{3}$ through the stem at the point where you wish the roots to form. Dust the cut with hormone powder, surround it with damp sphagnum moss, bind with polythene and secure with cellophane tape. When roots have formed, the layer can be cut away. The old plant should be nursed and will then provide a further supply of youngsters.

Air layering is the right treatment for the India-rubber plant that has lost its bottom leaves and charm.

2

3

It may be beheaded from the ripened wood below the second hard joint.

This method can also be tried on the plant that is failing; if not left too late, the leader may be transformed into a lively cutting.

### Offsets
Young growths that arrive around a plant are known as offsets and should be treated as cuttings or rooted cuttings. The pick-a-back plant and some others send out plantlets on their leaves on the end of special runners.

### Division
A mature plant may have its tufts or crowns gently pulled and teased apart in sections at potting time. This applies to the *marantas*, the aspidistra and the amaryllis bulb.

### Self-Propagation
Some plants, such as the *tradescantia*, never fail to root when their nodes touch damp soil. These rooted shoots have only to be detached to become independent.

### Vital Last Word
Keep cuttings damp — not wet — and the humidity as high as possible. If the leaves remain healthy while the roots are forming, they are doing well and the young plant is getting a fine send-off. The greatest danger is damping off and rot.

Cuttings and layers are amusing and wonderful experience. Surplus plants can go to friends or will

STEM CUTTING *2* — *cuttings ready to be planted.*

STEM CUTTING *3* — *cuttings planted next to the rim of the pot.*

sell like hot cakes at charity bazaars. Meanwhile the wise gardener with an eye to the future will succeed in keeping his collection on the young side.

Beyond this there is something particularly endearing about the home-grown plant.

# GROWING PLANTS FROM SEED

Growing seed in the house is not easy, but it is a stimulating experience for the novice to raise a plant and rather unenterprising if he does not experiment.

The obliging nasturtium will sprout in a pot in a dim corner and then grow up on a sunny window-sill, and I have seen *Cobaea scandens* and *ipomaea* (six in a 5-inch pot, later thinned to three plants) and *Asparagus plumosus* raised in much the same way. Warmth, moisture and air are the essentials.

Further seed worth trying: *Thunbergia alata* (the Black-eyed Susan vine), calendula, the marigold, always to be relied upon to make an effort, cineraria, mignonette, and Virginia stock.

The more temperamental plants require a propagating box; cacti demand a temperature around 70°F. if they are to germinate satisfactorily. Desirable bottom heat can be provided by placing the seed pan on a tray of moist gravel stationed on a moderately hot radiator.

### Notes for the Optimistic Seed-Grower

Use John Innes seed compost; if this is not available, mix a compost of 2 parts sterilized loam, 1 part peat and 1 part coarse sand passed through a ½-inch sieve. Add 1½ ounces super-phosphate of lime and ¾ ounce of powdered chalk to every bushel. Sow in a seed pan, box ('seed flat') or pot, paying great attention to cleanliness and crocking. The compost should now be put in and lightly firmed level, 1-inch below the top of the box or pot; the soil surface should then be given a generous sprinkling of sand. Finally soak the pan so that it will not require further watering before the seed has germinated.

Large, hard-skinned seeds should be soaked in tepid water 24 hours before sowing. Very tough skins are best notched with a nail file. Two seeds can be sown in a 4-inch pot; later the weakling may be discarded. Large seeds should be sown at least twice the depth of their diameter.

Small seeds should be thinly scattered; if mixed with sand they can be shaken from any suitable form of shaker, and will require no covering.

The beginner has a tendency to sow too thickly and too deep.

The seed pot should be covered with a sheet of glass to retain moisture; this should be lifted daily and wiped before condensation causes drip. A sheet of paper should be laid on top of the glass.

If the seeds are slow to germinate, the soil must be kept moist; bottom watering, by setting the flat in a tray of water, is the safest way. Moisture is of vital importance; dryness means certain death to seeds and seedlings; dampness without sogginess is what is wanted.

After sprouting, remove the paper covering and increase ventilation. Fresh air checks damping off. Once the seedlings have four leaves they can either be transplanted or thinned out. The throw-aways must be removed without disturbing their neighbours.

Seedlings do not always come up to expectations, but growing them is an excellent way of getting to know a plant and becoming a gardener. I still remember with affection my first crop of mustard and cress.

▶ THUNBERGIA ALATA — *this plant can be grown from seed.*

52

# PESTS AND DISEASES

Particular pests attack particular plants, and there are certain plants like the coleus that are mercilessly persecuted. But our homes are not wholly congenial to insect pests and the gardener should be able to check invasion. Cleanliness, spraying the occasional bath and plenty of fresh air will keep plants healthy and resistant. If prompt action is taken when the invader arrives, he can be controlled and defeated. But a badly damaged plant that has been ferociously attacked and has had its vitality sapped before being taken in hand is often better destroyed.

## PESTS

**Ants:** In sufficient numbers are capable of loosening the soil round roots.
*Treatment:*
Nippon dismisses them at once.

**Aphis:** With or without wings and in different colours, but all possessing six legs. Such a one may blow in your window and settle down, attacking young shoots or a fresh and tempting leaf. The leaves cockle and curl while the insects congregate on the undersides of the foliage. Greenfly attack nearly all plants, blackfly, the nasturtium and whitefly the geranium. The ant tastes the aphis' sweet secretion, known as honeydew, then carries the bug on to the next leaf or plant. I have often watched this well-organised traffic. Honeydew is often followed by a dirty sooty-mould fungus.
*Treatment:*
Spray or dust with derris or any reputable

contact insecticide. A sucking insect such as this is best eliminated by contact poison.

**Mealy Bug:** An oval, white fuzzy creature wrapped in a waxy grey-white substance that is waterproof. It haunts plant joints and hides against their spines, is one of the most common houseplant insects and the most destructive. Symptoms of its presence are yellow specks and general yellowing, deformity and a sick look. As this bug is a slow mover, it can be easily spotted and the sooner the better, for it is capable of laying 600 eggs at a time.
*Treatment:*
A swab or paint-brush dipped in a 50/50 spirit-and-water solution will kill instantaneously. When a root is affected by the mealy bug, the pudding should be knocked out and the affected parts painted with the spirit solution. Favourite victims are the cactus, saintpaulia, fuchsia and coleus. Alternatively, a sponge over with Volck will do the trick.

**Red Spider:** Scarlet or orange but so minute that it can seldom be seen by the naked eye. This

*Top.* ANTS — *in sufficient numbers are capable of loosening the soil round roots.*

▶ MEALY BUG — *the most common and destructive of houseplant insects.*

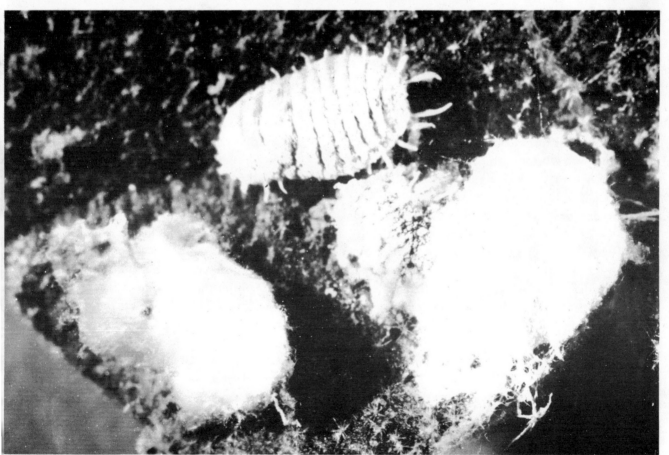

spider seeks plushy or hairy leaves, and thrives in a hot dry atmosphere. A regiment is capable of forming a white web, mottling the foliage yellow, scratching the leaves until they bleed. Is often found on the hydrangea.

*Treatment:*
Spray with soft-soap solution or Lindane, paying particular attention to the undersides of the leaves.

**Scale:** A large stationary insect with a brown-black armoured body. Likes the *hedera* family. Usually to be found on undersides of leaves.

*Treatment:*
Paint with methylated and water and allow the insect to dry. Then gently dislodge it.

**Thrips:** Is $\frac{1}{8}$-inch long and jumps about when hunted. The thrip spots the foliage, and can transform the leaves into paper skeletons. Attacks cyclamen.

*Treatment:*
Spray with D.D.T.

**Worm:** The worm upsets crocks and drainage and mildly annoys.

*Treatment:*
Water with weak mustard water and eject the worm.

**Uncommon Event:** Every now and then a caterpillar can be found on a rich green leaf; finger and thumb acts quicker than anything else.

## Do's and one Don't

**Do:** ● Take immediate action. Insects increase at prodigious speed. You can try a spray of soap and water before using anything stronger. It often does the job. Remember nicotine and H.E.T.P. are poisonous and should be kept under lock and key. They are not advised for the amateur. Derris is safe (for all but fish). Spray with clean water a few hours after treating with soap or insecticide. Use a syringe capable of allowing a strong driving mist. Direct contact is the thing.
● Follow the manufacturer's instructions to the letter.
● Buy healthy plants and so run no risk of infection.
● Inspect regularly, even after the 'all clear'.
● Watch out for the return of a survivor!

**Don't** Bring unhealthy plants in contact with the healthy.

**Comfort.** If you keep your plants clean and growing healthily you may never be bothered, or visited. Insects and disease attack the ill-conditioned.

## Diseases

Ill health is usually the lot of the plant dissatisfied with its environment. If conditions are not to its liking, all sorts of disorders and ugly secondary symptoms may present themselves. It is no easier for a gardener than a doctor to diagnose a complaint. The novice is confused by the fact that the same out-of-sorts appearance may be caused by over- or under-watering, overfeeding or starvation. Turning out the pot will help him to form his judgment.

Here is my novice's quiz:
● Overwatering
● Waterlogging — is the drainage hole free?
● Is the pot standing in a saucerful of water?
● Have you watered the plant with cold tap water (during the winter)?
● Have you overwatered during the winter or resting time?
● Is the plant too dry?
● Have you allowed it at any time to dry out?
● Does the plant get enough light?
● Has it stood in the hot midday sun? Has the pot been sunbaked?
● Is the soil exhausted? — or sour?
● Is the plant overfed? Have you given too much fertilizer, or given it too often?
● Or overfed a plant with fertilizer during the resting period? When dry?
● Or overfed the unestablished or ailing plant — the newcomer?
● Is the plant suffering from a dry atmosphere?
● Is it too near the fire or radiator?
● Is it in a draught?
● Is it too cold at night on the window-sill?
● Is it on the cold side of the curtains?

It is hoped the above quiz will help the owner to discover what is wrong with the plant and perhaps his own besetting sin.

## The new Plant

The gardener must be patient with the new plant and allow it reasonable time to acclimatize; it will settle down far quicker in the summer than the winter. Smaller leaves, yellowing, a fall of leaf and a de-

▶ *An arrangement consisting of* RHOICISSUS RHOMBOIDEA, CHLOROPHYTUM CAPENSE VAR *and* HEDERA.

▼ IPOMEA — *a climbing plant with large blue trumpet-shaped flowers.*

◄ *An attractive container with an arrangement of* PHILO-
DENDRON SCANDENS, DRACAENA TERMINALIS, HEDERA
'LITTLE DIAMOND', HEDERA 'GREEN RIPPLE, DRACAENA
GODSEFFIANA *and* BEGONIA REX. *The arrangement in the
right hand corner includes* RHOICISSUS RHOMBOIDEA, PEPE-
ROMIA CAPERATA *and* SANSEVIERIA. *A* PEPEROMIA
MAGNOLIAEFOLIA *and* GYNURA SARMENTOSA *are shown
on the left of the picture.*

▼ *The plant on the left of the picture is an* APHELANDRA
SILVER BEAUTY. *The tallest plant on the right is a* PHILO-
DENDRON SCANDENS, *next to which is a* HEDERA CANA-
RIENSIS. *In the corner is a* PEPEROMIA MAGNOLIAEFOLIA,
SAINTPAULIA *and* SEDUM SIEBOLDII.

pressed appearance may be expected. Cosset the new-comer for a month or so until it is acclimatized, but don't over-pamper.

## DISEASES

**Damping Off:** The stems weaken and wilt at soil level and the plants topple over. Seedlings are vulnerable. The trouble may be due to fungus but is more often caused by extremes of temperature, draughts, bad ventilation or careless watering.
*Treatment:*
Rotted leaves or stems should be removed and burnt. Infected soil should be replaced or can be treated with a Cheshnut Compound.

**Fungus Spot:** A growth of brown spots and rotted flesh in cacti and succulents. Possibly due to excessive moisture.
*Treatment:*
Application of a solution of Bordeaux mixture. Rotted parts may be cut away from cacti and succulents and dusted with flowers of sulphur.

**Mildew:** A whitish powder on the leaves; a sign of excessive dampness, overcrowding or lack of ventilation.
*Treatment:*
Dust with flowers of sulphur, or spray with Karathane, improve ventilation and water with extra care.

**Mould and Moss:** Caused by a constantly damp condition.
*Treatment:*
Scrape away moss or sour soil, replace with fresh compost and pay attention to soil aeration.

**Wilting:** Check with quiz (see page 56) and try to discover the reason.

**Yellowing, spindly and inferior growth:** Yellowing may be due to lack of nitrogen in the soil but is usually caused by lack of light, over-watering, overfeeding, dry roots or exhausted soil. In the case of distorted or damaged leaves the disfigurement may be due to aphis or pests (see page 54).
*Treatment:*
Check with the quiz (see page 56). Give the plant a light position. Apply a nitrogen fertilizer if general treatment fails.

**Sudden leaf fall:** Brought about by sudden change

of conditions, draught, gas fumes, unsuitable watering and cold tap-water in the winter, or possibly too much hot sun. The temporary complaint of the newcomer.
*Treatment:*
Check with quiz (see page 56) and act accordingly.

**Dry Spots, Ugly Margins and Patches:** Over-watering is often the cause of the disfigurement. Check with quiz (see page 56) and correct any shortcoming.

**Bud and Flower Drop:** This may be due to over-watering, dryness at roots, dry atmosphere, too much sun or a fluctuating temperature. It should be remembered that a plant requires more water while in bud and flower. Certain plants (the Christmas Cactus among them) resent being moved and the direction of light changed at this important time.
*Treatment:*
Extra careful watering, and a halt to pot turning.

**Variegated plant that reverts to green:** The variegated subjects are slower growing and appear more sensitive to conditions than their fellows. Delicate variegation is by no means steadfast, whereas reversion to green is usually constant as everyone who has grown the elusive purple-flushed *tradescantia* will know.
*Treatment:*
Plants must be given a light position. But whereas bright light is essential to them, too strong a light may turn white variegation an unsatisfactory yellow.
The unwanted green shoots that so often appear on the variegated *tradescantia* should be pinched out.

**Collapse:** May be caused by frost, baking in the sun, gas fumes, desert dryness or waterlogging.
*Treatment:*
A frozen plant should be put in a cool, dark place where it can slowly thaw out. It may be watered with cold water. The extremely dry can be soaked in a bucket: if the water rushes through the pot without being absorbed, prick the soil with a knitting needle. The water-logged may be allowed to dry out at its own pace. It may be syringed if flagging. When on inspecting the roots new white rootlets are visible, moderate watering may begin.

## Two Warnings.

1. The sick plant goes downhill fast; cut off the top leader and transform it into a cutting before it is too late. (See Air-layering, page 50).
2. Wash your hands with soapy water after handling a diseased plant or you may spread infection.

**Comfort** Nursing a failing plant will teach you a lot.

## Last Word on Culture

Success with house plants will depend upon attention to detail. Plant watching is entertaining and if you tend your plants every day you will get to know them and keep them far longer. You'll find they prefer normal fare and few excesses.

Indoor gardening requires experience and skill. It is not enough to keep a plant alive; a sickly plant is a depressing companion. The wood must be a live colour, the leaves a perfect green, and the flower buds bursting with health and impatient to bloom.

*Top left.* APHIS — *will attack leaves, causing them to cockle and curl.*

*Above.* RED SPIDER — *seeks plush or hairy leaves, and thrives in a hot, dry atmosphere.*

▼ SCALE INSECTS — *large stationary insect usually found on underside of leaves.*

# PART TWO

## EIGHTEEN "EASIES"

# EIGHTEEN "EASIES"

**ALOE**

A succulent with stiff spiky rosettes, some of the family being too big for house plants.

**A. arborescens** the torch, a slow grower.

**A. plicatilis** is greyish, 8—12-inches across but up to 10 ft. high. A neat plant when healthy; at other times a misery.

**A. variegata,** Partridge-breasted Aloe, Mackerel Cactus, or Tiger Aloe, is dark green speckled white and engagingly banded. This is the show piece of the family with loose spikes of orange-red flowers in spring. The Germans are particularly fond of this stubby small plant, about 12-in. high, native of South Africa.

I possess a Partridge-breasted Aloe that has stood up to the roughest of treatment during my absence from home, so I am biased in its favour.

The aloe likes a sandy loam, peat and well-rotted manure, a sunny position and mild doses of fertilizer from April onwards. It should be kept cool and dry through the winter, being well accustomed to drought. Perfect drainage is essential.

*Propagation:* by offsets with at least 5 leaves from the base of the plant and cuttings. These should be given 48 hours to callus before being inserted in a sandy leafmould mixture.

**ARAUCARIA**

**A. excelsa** is a conifer with the look of the Christmas tree and is the Norfolk Island Pine. Attractive when young as a table plant, its branches appear in tiers and it was no doubt its stiff bearing that appealed to the Victorians. I include it in my eighteen for novices, not only because I think it too little known by the present generation but also because there is none better for the cool-to-cold room where the gardener is away all day. The plant is practically hardy and at my old home in Berkshire in a sheltered spot there is a thriving **A. cunninghamii** (Moreton Bay Pine) of over 50 feet that many years ago was dismissed from the glasshouse because it was too tall. Provided the plant is kept cool (not more than 60 °F. in winter) and out of the draught, it is nearly foolproof.

*Culture*

Soil: good ordinary soil — 2 parts loam, 1 part leaf-mould, 1 part silver sand. Re-pot or top dress in March. Water sparingly in winter, freely in summer with an occasional syringe. The *araucaria* likes air and elbow room, and for this reason is better not included in a group arrangement.

*Propagation:* summer cuttings are best struck in mild heat, but are not easy. If the *araucaria* loses its lower branch tiers it becomes an ugly sight and should be decapitated and the top treated as a cutting (see page 48).

▶ ALOE VARIEGATA *(partridge-breasted aloe)* — *has loose spikes of orange-red flowers in spring.*

## ASPARAGUS

This is the lace-like foliage plant, beloved of the florist. Surprisingly a member of the lily group, and often seen in a bouquet or basket.

**A. asparagoides,** synonym of *A. medesloides*, a plant of the lily family.

**A. plumosus,** upright and feathery, evergreen climber.

**A. sprengeri,** emerald feather, climber, 2—6 feet. The best asparagus for the house. Has needle-like leaves and small white fragrant flowers appear on the adult plant, followed by red berries. There is also the rather unsatisfactory variegated form.

These are all greedy feeders enjoying a rich loam and leaf-mould with a sand content, and doses of liquid manure when fully established. They are humidity lovers, and should be given a spray and plenty of water when growing. Desirable winter temperature about 55 degrees F. The plant is happy in partial shade and must be kept out of the hot sun or the foliage will discolour.

A mangy asparagus is a horrid sight; it should be cut back ruthlessly in the hope that it will break anew.

*Propagation:* by seed and cuttings.

## ASPIDISTRA

This plant has a long history. It was prized by the Victorians and then, becoming a music hall joke, thrown out by the Edwardians along with the antimacassars and pictures of Highland cattle.

A slow grower it is now making a fast comeback, is difficult to find and expensive to buy. The flower

arrangers, realising the value of the dark green oblong foliage, are willing to pay 4—5s. a leaf. These wear well and, having served their purpose in a number of summer arrangements, may be painted and used for Christmas decorations.

The aspidistra is a plant of great longevity and will survive for decades without feeding or re-potting. There are still venerable specimens about and I know of two planted in Georgian mahogany wine-coolers that are treated as treasured heirlooms.

It will be some time before the house plant nurseryman will be able to build up a stock of the aspidistra, meanwhile, anyone lucky enough to find one for private sale will be expected to pay an impressive sum for it.

The variegated aspidistra with cream stripes is an extremely handsome subject. Flowers from all forms are insignificant and, appearing at soil level, often pass unnoticed.

*Culture*

This plant has an iron constitution and can stand up to drought, fluctuating temperatures, dark corners and draughts. It should be kept in the semi-shade during the summer otherwise the leaves may discolour. Beyond this, cultural instruction is superfluous except for ample watering.

*Propagation:* split up gently when re-potting in March.

## ASPLENIUM

A large number of fern species can be grown in cool rooms provided the novice inquires about the demands and habits of the fern he is buying and leaves *adiantum*, the elegant maidenhair, to the more experienced. Those with the hard fronds are the easiest and here are three of the really co-operative:

**A. bulbiferum,** the mother or New Zealand spleenwort, is the beginner's fern with an immaculate indoor reputation. The young plantlets that form on the juicy and finely divided fronds from which further plants can be propagated are an added entertainment and excellent experience.

**A. nidus.** Having gained confidence the novice can then move on to this slightly more fussy but very beautiful Bird's-nest Fern, sometimes known as the Shuttlecock. Its bearing and shining green leaves, brown ribbed and fluted, make it most desirable.

**A. Pteris.** This crested fern is popular, particularly with the butchers, who frequently leave it to furnish

▲ ASPIDISTRA — *a plant of great longevity and will survive for decades without feeding or re-potting.*

*Left.* ASPARAGUS SPRENGERI — *has needle-like leaves and small white fragrant flowers appear on the adult plant.*

▶ ASPARAGUS PLUMROSUS — *an upright and feathery evergreen climber.*

65

▶ CHLOROPHYTUM CAPENSE VARIEGATUM, *the Spider Plant — has rosettes of pale green and cream grass-like leaves.*

their empty window and plates over the weekend. My butcher has had his handsome uncomplaining *pteris* for over five years, and it is looking handsome as ever.

There are 6,000 fern species to choose from, but only a very limited number of these will consent to live in the house. Hardy ferns found on a country walk seldom survive indoors.

*Culture*

Soil: 1 part loam, 2 parts peat, 1 part silver sand, a lump of charcoal and a dash of bone meal. Pot in March (avoid overpotting). Moisture-loving *A. nidus* has an insatiable summer thirst: revels in a syringe but resents water in its saucer. Protection must be given from strong sunlight; if fronds turn yellow the fern may be moved to a north window until re-covered.

*Propagation:* by division when re-potting. Avoid tight planting by using light fingers and an open mixture.

## CHLOROPHYTUM

**Chlorophytum capense variegatum** (botanically known as *C. comosum*), the Spider Plant, has the gift of adapting itself to almost anybody's home. This is one of the oldest house plants and in 1828 was greatly admired by the poet Goethe. It is a gift to the beginner. It possesses rosettes of pale green and cream grass-like leaves, and is quite a satisfactory hanging plant, especially when, after flowering, the new and small plantlets weigh down and arch the lemon stalks. This is the plant's fascinating manner of reproducing itself.

*Culture*

This easy-going South African likes a rich light soil of J.I.P. No. 2. Allow plenty of space for watering when potting; this margin will be quickly filled with roots. It should be watered freely in summer and little in winter. The plant likes a bright position but should be kept out of the hot sun as the leaves are apt to get brittle. It is an excellent basket plant, but beware of greenfly.

*Propagation:* by division or even more simply by pegging the dangling plantlets in a pot of sandy compost and later detaching them from the parent.

## CISSUS ANTARCTICA

This is the easy-going Kangaroo Vine, a relation of the Virginia Creeper, a native of Australia and a decorative evergreen climber with good firm stems.

I have no hesitation in recommending it to anyone with a modern built-in trough who wishes to grow a green screen between the kitchen and dining-room. It will swarm up a string or cane or make its way in and out of a trellis at the comfortable rate of 2—3 feet a year. Its tendrils enable it to cling to the wall with a minimum number of drawing pins — that is, if you do not mind puncturing plaster and paper. This plant needs a masterful gardener with a firm hand if it is to be trained and seen at its best. If a climber does not fit in with the decor, the top shoot can be pinched out and the result will soon be a bushy semi-creeper or trailer. Its curly tendrils and vine-like habit make it most adaptable.

The shiny serrated oval-shaped leaves are not

a moderately cool place; will put up with an unheated room if it is frost-proof. Enjoys good light but requires protection from bright sun. At a pinch it can manage with very little light.

Use the watering-can liberally during the summer when the plant is growing rapidly, but let it almost dry out between waterings. This is an important point that must be carefully watched during the winter, when the water supply should be cut down. A number of gardeners complain that their plants look sick with either drooping foliage or leaves with brown patches from November on; in most cases the trouble is due to over-watering. So water sparingly once the days begin to shorten. Weak and occasional doses of any reputable fertilizer will be welcome during the summer. Prune in the spring if fresh green shoots are wanted.

Plants may take a little time to settle down in a new home; they are conservative about surroundings, resenting abrupt changes in treatment and gardener.

*Propagation:* by layering or spring cuttings.

## CLIVIA

The Kaffir Lily, an evergreen from South Africa, large and rather grand, suitable for tubs and large rooms. The leaves are fleshy and strap-like: the umbels of orange flowers are borne on thick stems during late spring or summer and have a beautiful scent.

*Culture*

Soil: a rich leafmould and loam, and doses of fertilizer when flowering. Likes to be almost potbound and is an unwilling transplanter. Best moved in February when almost dry. Adores the sun and a south window, but care should be taken that the leaves do not get burned. Must be encouraged to take its winter rest if expected to flower; cut down the water supply from August onwards. Top dress when the plant wakes up. The *clivia* will benefit by a summer in the garden.

*Propagation:* by seed, which should be sown immediately when ripe, otherwise it may not germinate; also by young offsets.

## CRASSULA

It is desirable that the beginner should get to know a few succulents. They are decorative, make excellent house plants and are, on the whole, easy; they enjoy dry air and do not call for extra humidity that so many indoor plants look upon as a necessity.

unlike those of the beech; they are a lovely fresh green and the veins on the undersides are tinted red.

In Denmark I found the *Cissus antarctica* constantly used as a green archway between two rooms.

**Rhoicissus rhomboidea,** with silver buds and tendrils, is another easy evergreen vine that is bound to please.

**C. discolor** is a highly decorative trailer that needs support if it is to be grown upright. It requires a very much warmer temperature than *C. antarctica* (at least 55°F. in winter) and is altogether more demanding — apt to shed its leaves if discontented.

*Culture*

Soil: J.I.P. No. 2 with an addition of peat and leafmould is a favourite diet, but any good soil will do. Pot April—May. Likes an east or west window and

I have a warm corner in my heart for **C. arborea,** the Japanese rubber plant or jade tree with spoon-shaped leaves. A gardening friend of mine bought a minute 'shelf plant' at a store some years ago. It is now an imposing tree-like plant in a 60 pot, and flowered white and fragrant last year. It has never been fussed over. Others to look out for are **C. lycopodioides;** with tiny flowers in the axils of their leaves so small that they often pass unnoticed. Perfect for dish gardens and once at home will grow rapidly. **C. teres,** a little more pernickety than the others, is on a short slender column with leaves so close that they form an almost smooth surface. **C. rupestris:** prostrate, grey-green with brown dots and margin and small yellow flowers. Lastly **C. falcata,** that grows up to 3 feet with fleshy sickle-shaped leaves, opposite each other, embracing and hiding the stem, and has clusters of carmine flowers.

*Culture*

Soil: a rich sandy gritty mixture with an addition of crushed brick or mortar rubble and a lump of charcoal, or J.I.P. No. 2 plus crushed or Cornish grit, and a surface layer of pebbles and chips to keep the base of the plants dry. Re-pot March; a change of soil every 2 years is a sound plan. Water moderately during the summer while the plants are growing and only just enough to keep them from drying out through the winter, and not a drop more, for they are vulnerable to rot. Succulents always seem happy in a south window close to the pane. Keep them on the inside of the curtain on a cold night. So long as the temperature does not fall below 40°F. they are safe.

*Propagation:* by seed, cuttings or leaf cuttings.

## FICUS ELASTICA DECORA

The fig or India-rubber belongs to an important house plant family with more than 1,000 members. *F. elastica decora* is an improvement upon *F. elastica* that was so much seen in the Victorian Aspidistra Age. Its dignified, straight stem and decisive line have won favour with architects and decorators, and the modern shop-window dresser would be lost without it. It looks well as a solitary plant standing on the floor — towering up to the ceiling. The large leaves with veined dark red undersides are well formed and the small plant with the top leaf still wrapped in a red-pink sheath is a useful background member in a group. If the plant is in good heart, the sheath will be a reddish colour. But if stationed in a dark corner it will be pale and pinkish. The sheath protects the new

▶ FICUS TRICOLOUR — *the leaves of this plant are marked silver-grey and cream and have an attractive pink midrib.*

▼ CLIVIA — *an evergreen from South Africa, with fleshy leaves; it has orange flowers, with a beautiful scent, during late spring or summer.*

leaf and will fall off when the new one matures; is should not be pulled off until it has completed its protective function.

Sometimes when a plant is bought staked, the fading sheath is held against the new leaf, too tight and too long, and this can lead to the rotting of the vulnerable new leaf.

The imperturbable *F. elastica decora* is almost fool-proof.

**F. doescheri** (a variegated form of the old elastica). This plant requires more light than its predecessors. Is more temperamental and particularly vulnerable to over-watering.

**F. pumila** is another beginner's plant. It is an attractive small climber with close-set papery leaves and aerial rootlets. A good plant for a cold room. In certain parts of the country it survives outside.

*Propagation:* by shoots.

**F. schryveriana.** This Ficus is quite tough, of yellow and green colouring and with smaller leaves than decora.

**F. tricolour.** A lovely newcomer from the Continent, is a sport from *Ficus decora*. The leaves are marked silver-grey and cream and have an attractive pink midrib.

*Culture*

Soil: rich leafmould with a dash of sand or J.I.P. No. 2. Pot March—April. Once the plant has settled down, it may be fed. It should be placed in a good light but not in the full sun, kept moist but not wet and given fewer drinks in the winter when resting. Discoloration of leaves is often the result of over-

◄ HEDERA GLACIER — *one of the best trailing plants.*

► FICUS TRICOLOUR.

*Below right.* FICUS DOESCHERI — *a variegated form of the Ficus elastica decora.*

watering. *F. pumila* is the exception that needs water the whole year through and must never be allowed to dry out. Young plants require staking.

*F. elastica decora* has a strong constitution, but sometimes loses its lower leaves and good appearance. It should then be air layered (see page 50). The gardener must be prepared for a gush of white sticky latex from any wound of the stem; this must be immediately bound with adhesive tape to save the plant distress and weakness, and the gardener the milky overflow and mess.

## HEDERA

The *hedera* or ivy is one of the most widely grown house plants and now, with the introduction of attractive new varieties, is leaving the *tradescantia* far behind. It will hang, trail or climb without much care or encouragement but responds to good compost and a regular wash and wipe.

This plant likes a cool, light place. The Americans find it difficult to grow because their rooms are too hot. In the States the English Ivy is respected and treasured.

Here is my choice from some 700 species:

**H. helix adam:** A miniature newcomer. It is a grey-cream variegation with small leaves and is self-branching at nearly every leaf joint. It likes it cool and can survive a low temperature.

**H. helix canariensis variegata:** Is not quite so hardy as the rest of the family and resents over-watering in the winter. The leaves should flag slightly before watering in the winter and the plant must not

71

▲ HEDERA HELIX ADAM — *a grey-cream variegation with small leaves, and is self-branching at nearly every leaf joint. It likes the cool and can survive a low temperature.*

be over-potted. It is a cream and green plant with leaves of leathery texture and red stems: slow and slightly tender, requiring more warmth and sun than green ivy.

**H. helix cristata or holly:** Frilled leaves like parsley. Easy to grow and grips congenial surfaces. Should be kept a little drier than its colleagues.

**H. helix glacier:** One of the best of the trailers. White-edged and charming.

**H. helix golden jubilee:** A delightful German introduction. Small golden leaves with wide dark-green margin. I have a large plant of golden jubilee and am delighted with it.

**H. helix Pittsburgh:** Small leaves with faint white veins and a graceful trailer. Clings rather than climbs.

**H. helix sagittaefolia:** An improvement on Pittsburgh. Very pointed leaves. Good bushy and trailing habit.

**Hedera standards grafted on Fatshedera stock:** Ivy standards of three to four feet tall are likely to become popular, but by no means common as they take some years to mature to three or four feet which is the ideal.

The practice is to cut back the fatshedera at the top of the plant, making a cross cut half an inch deep. Four ivy cuttings of four inches in length (with about five leaves) can be inserted in the cut and bound up. A polythene bag should then be placed over the cuttings and the top of the fatshedera stem so that the cuttings are kept air-tight for eight or ten weeks when signs of life should be visible.

If you have failed in the past with house plants, try ivy. I've known it survive gas fumes and the roughest of gardeners.

*Culture*

Our wild ivy seems to prefer alkaline and limey soil to acid peat: so put a sprinkling of hydrated lime in the compost. On the other hand, an addition of peat will hold the desired moisture and many knowledgeable gardeners grow plants in a mixture of peat and sand or John Innes. Ivy isn't difficult if it is kept moist without being soggy through the summer months and never allowed to dry out. The water supply should be cut down from October to March. Yellow leaves usually mean that more drink, humidity or food is needed (a saucer of wet pebbles or a spray if the atmosphere is very dry).

Although the ivy can manage without much light the happy plant will space its leaves with becoming regularity while the one in the dark corner gives an

▲ HEDERA CANARIENSIS VARIEGATA — *a cream and green plant with leaves of leathery texture and red stems. This is a slow and slightly tender plant, requiring more warmth and sun than the green ivy.*

uneven performance. It is advisable to keep the pot in the shade on a hot summer's day.

*Propagation:* the tip of a shoot will root in water or soil without any trouble. A rooted stem can be imported from a tree base, woods or hedgerows. There are any number of varieties of our own wild ivy, so pick one with a prettily patterned leaf and bushy habit. Some of them will and some of them won't acclimatize themselves to your home. But they are, after all, gift horses.

## HELXINE

Irish or Japanese Moss, Baby's Tears, or just Mind Your Own Business is a delightful low growing little creeper from Corsica and Sardinia. It has tiny round leaves on the thinnest of stems, a moss-like appearance and is most frequently seen carpeting the ground beneath the glasshouse staging.

*Helxine* is a relation of the nettle and a most useful house plant; not only will it carpet a single plant or a group, but it will also form an immaculate green cushion on its own, quickly covering the surface of a shallow pan. Clinging to the soil, it will neither creep nor trail far beyond the pot. Gardeners may care to build up a pyramid or green fountain with this small plant. This is done by filling 3—4 size-graded pots with soil and sinking them into each other: the margins can then be planted with divided plants and cuttings.

The yellow *helxine* is seldom seen. I found it growing in Denmark, where it had been imported from Kew. I now have a fragment growing in the kitchen where it revels in the steam from the kettle.

*Culture*

Soil: leafmould, loam and sand or J.I.P. No. 1. The plant has no fads and fancies other than a strong dislike of gas fumes and a love of moisture. Grows well in partial shade and a north window. It prefers a cool temperature of about 45 to 55°F.; impossible to kill unless allowed to go thirsty.

*Propagation:* by division; will grow from fragments in the spring.

## PELARGONIUM

This is the geranium, often superbly grown by the cottager.

Few seem to be aware of the many lovely varieties that exist both old and new. The gardener is advised to send for a *pelargonium* specialist's catalogue and to break fresh ground. Paul Crampel and Gustave Emich are good scarlets but they have been greatly overworked. The Geranium Society (10s. subscription) brings out quarterly and annual bulletins for the geranium fan.

The zonal list is a long one. I am particularly devoted to Lady Folkestone, a single blush pink with a splendid temperament. For the novice, there is L'Elegante, an ivy-leaf with leaves that have white and mauve variegation; the flowers are creamy white with purple markings and are of secondary importance.

The fragrant-leaved species, **Citrodorum,** Prince of Orange, and **Tomentosum** with its clear peppermint scent and velvety leaves, are all too seldom seen. The magnificent Washington group, **P. domesticum,** pansy-shaped with the two top petals in most cases blotched in a darker and richer shade, are the belles of the family but are more difficult to grow and have a shorter flowering season.

The geranium is not exacting but must have sunlight. It is a particularly cheerful flower and blooms from May to October.

*Culture*

Soil: 1 part leafmould, 2 parts loam, 1 part sharp sand and an addition of dried cow manure and a sprinkling of bonemeal. Pot May.

The gardener must decide whether he wants his plants to flower in the winter or summer; they cannot do both.

If the winter bloom is desired, the flower buds must be picked off as soon as they appear, until October. If summer bloom is wished for, the plants should be re-potted and cut back in October and allowed to rest through the winter.

Some gardeners put their plants in a dark cellar for the resting period; any frost-proof place where the temperature does not fall below 40°F. will do. Return the plants to the sunny window-sill in May.

The geranium is sun-loving, drinks copiously during the summer when flowering, after which it likes a quiet rest. Keep your stock young; old plants become leggy, unattractive and beyond repair, often losing courage and ceasing to flower. The geranium flowers best when almost pot-bound. A fortnightly dose of a general fertilizer from June onwards will help to keep a plant vigorous, but over-generous feeding may lead to all foliage and no flowers.

*Propagation:* cuttings can be taken any time be-

▶ CLIVIA MINIATA — *an evergreen from South Africa with umbels of orange flowers.*

*(Page 76) An arrangement showing* FICUS BENJAMINA, DIEFFENBACHIA EXOTICA, DIEFFENBACHIA AMOENA, SANSEVIERIA TRIFASCIATA LAURENTII, CROTON, CROTON 'VOLCANO' *and* PLEOMELE REFLEXA PICTA.

◄ *The plant on the window sill is a* SAINTPAULIA CAVA-LIER. *The arrangement consists of* FICUS BENJAMINA, DRACAENA TERMINALIS, SANSEVIERIA TRIFASCIATA LAU-RENTII *and* HEDERA ADAM.

*(Page 77) The tall plant is a* FICUS ELASTICA DECORA — *a plant from a family with more than 1,000 members. In the right hand corner is a* PODOCARPUS SINUATUS, *and* NEANTHE BELLA. *The plant at the back is a* CYCLAMEN SILVER LEAF *and to the left of the picture is a* HEDERA GREEN RIPPLE *and* HEDERA CHICAGO VARIEGATA.

tween May and October provided they are given shade. Firm and mature shoots should be selected and cut below the third or fourth joint, the lower leaves and any wings removed, keeping only two or three leaves. Let the shoots lie in a cool, airy place for 24 hours before insertion. Water after inserting and then keep the soil just moist until the cuttings perk up and grow. This should happen in 2 weeks.

## PHILODENDRON SCANDENS

This plant is my pick of the house plants for the novice. It is a fast, uncomplaining climber, almost pest-free and an excellent plant for a dark room, managing with a minimum of light. Easy and decorative, it wins favour wherever it grows. Meanwhile there is said to be a *philodendron* in one of every two bathrooms in the States. This is a member of an important house plant family, a quick grower with glossy, rather leathery, but utterly delightful heart-shaped leaves. Primarily a climber that with the aid of a string or cane (it must have support) will travel the curtain and pelmet with the ease with which it mounts a tree in the jungle. If you wrap the cane with moss and keep this padding damp, the journey will be made more comfortable and 20 feet covered in no time.

Some gardeners train plants up the wall against which the leaves lie flat and effectively patterned, held in place with drawing pins; that is, if you do not mind puncturing plaster and paper.

On the other hand, for a bushy plant, pinch out the leader; then provide a piece of moist cork bark to which aerial shoots can cling and you will be rewarded by thick and luxuriant foliage. Shoots may also be trailed along the edge of a trough or basket to break the line.

The flower, a calla-shaped bloom of no particular interest or beauty, is seldom seen.

The *philodendrons* come from South and Central America. A number of them will grow in our homes, but not so contentedly as **P. scandens.** Here are a few:

**P. andreanum** is a slender climber with small 5—6 inch leaf, dark green velvet texture with pale-purple-pink undersides. Very beautiful but temperamental.

**P. bipinnatifidum** has large glossy leaves as much as 15 inches across.

**P. bipennifolium** has 3 lobed glossy leaves, the centre lobe being outstandingly long. Hardy, easy and much

beloved in Germany.

**P. burgundy.** A newcomer with deep, wine-red stem which is reflected in the graceful shiny leaves.

**P. leichtlinii** is fussy, but has interesting leaves slashed more evenly than those of *Monstera deliciosa*.

*Culture*

John Innes No. 2 with a sprinkling of sand is a favourite diet. A winter temperature of 60°—70°F. is ideal. The plant will not stand the very cold and dislikes a hot dry atmosphere, but is on the whole remarkably reasonable. Water freely in summer and more sparingly in the winter: an occasional spray is welcomed, and please don't let the leaves get grimy.

Re-pot or top dress with a rich mixture of peat, leafmould and sand or John Innes No. 2.

*Propagation:* cuttings of 4—5 inches will root easily in sandy soil or water during the spring.

## SANSEVIERIA

If its stiff appearance appeals and you are looking for a die-hard, the Snake Plant or Bow-string Hemp will suit you. **S. laurentii,** a variety of *S. trifasciata* from the Congo is the star turn of a large family with 3—4 foot long sword-shaped leaves, mottled and margined with yellow. This is what the Americans describe as an accent plant; a slow grower, useful in a trough arrangement providing an erect and striking silhouette. It will stand up to anything except overwatering in the winter. Can tolerate long periods of drought. Nickname? Mother-in-law's Tongue. So indestructible! It flowers on occasion, generally when

▲ PELARGONIUM — *the geranium, a cheerful flower that blooms from May to October.*

*Left.* PEPEROMIA GLABELLA — *variety of peperomia.*

pot-bound; scented greenish-yellow summer blooms on leafless stalks.

*Culture*

Soil: J.I.P. No. 2 or a sandy mixture with little organic matter. Pot March or April. The *sansevieria* seems to prefer neglect to fussing and likes to be pot-bound. If it feels uncomfortably cramped it may crack the pot. Use the can sparingly even in the summer and scarcely at all during the winter. Keep the foliage clean. This is a desert plant that tolerates shade but prefers the sun.

*Propagation:* by division and 3-inch cuttings. These sections should be dried off, planted in sand and are best taken during the spring. Have a care that they are planted the right way up with the cut edge which was nearest the root inserted in the soil. Unfortunately young plants from cuttings will not reproduce the attractive yellow margins but revert to the dark green and duller *S. trifasciata.*

## SAXIFRAGA SARMENTOSA

This is the strawbery geranium or Mother of Thousands, an almost hardy cold-room plant. It has rounded reddish marbled leaves and panicles of long-lasting white-pink flowers in the late spring or summer.

The runners that spring from the rosette of the

plant hang over the edge of the pot in an attractive manner. A useful basket subject or trailer from an elevated pot. The variegated form 'tricolor' with pink and cream leaves is attractive but not so free and easy.

*Culture*

Any good open soil of loam, leafmould and sand is suitable. The plant likes a cool temperature, not much above 50°F., to be protected from bright sunshine and watered freely in the summer.

*Propagation:* the strawberry-like runners should be started in May and given a large enough pot for rosettes to develop (about 3 inches).

## TRADESCANTIA

It can be argued that the *tradescantia* named after Charles I's gardener, John Tradescanti, is the best-tempered house plant we possess. Sometimes known as the Travelling Sailor, we know it better as the Wandering Jew that travels far and wide.

It is not a climber but makes a willing basket subject, trailing sometimes as much as 2—3 feet. In an arrangement and medley of plants, it is helpful in camouflaging the bare or bald appearance of a less buoyant companion. A plant lifted on a down-turned pot will hang and look well.

There are a number of varieties of this genus owing to considerable intermarriage in the family.

**T. blossfeldiana:** Glossy leaves with purple undersides.

**T. fluminensis aurea:** Green with yellow stripes.

**T. fluminensis variegata:** Green with white stripes.

**T. albiflora:** Small green leaves, mauve shading. A plant that often surprises its owner by flowering.

**T. tricolour:** Green, pink-mauve and white markings.

**Zebrina pendula** (*T. zebrina*): Grey with mauve striped foliage. Fast grower.

**Zebrina purpusii:** Dark mauve. Largish leaves.

The pink-mauve flowers of the *tradescantia* are of secondary importance.

To retain the delightful pink tinge of the foliage, the plant must be given a light position and kept on the dry side. Some leaves are colourful while others are pale and almost translucent.

There is no difficulty in buying this easy-going plant and it is cheap. The silver-and-white variety has a fragile look but is tough.

*Culture*

This is a plant that will take what it is given, but enjoys any good all-round open compost with a dash of sand. A dejected plant will look altogether rejuvenated if potted in John Innes.

It needs constant watering in summer and can be safely soaked under the tap and left in the sink to drain. In the winter it benefits by a rest and requires just enough water to keep it alive.

The position of the plant is important. The variation in colouring will depend on whether the foliage is in sun or shade: the proportion of cream, silver, red and purple in the papery transparent leaves will vary accordingly. In a shady corner it may acquire profuse foliage but will remain an unexciting green. Try to find a half-way house for it; not too sunny but in a sufficiently bright place to bring out the desirable pink tinge.

I have yet to meet anyone who has killed a *tradescantia*, but it is easy to let your plant go downhill and there are far too many leggy and miserable specimens about. The plant must be kept trimmed and busy. An ungainly trailer can be re-rooted in the pot and the shoots that have reverted to plain green must be ruthlessly pinched out or they will oust the variegation. Plants should be treated with care when dusting; it is invariably the wrong shoot that gets broken off. Temperature is not a problem. *Tradescantia* likes warmth, will put up with cold but not frost.

*Propagation:* a leaf will be found at every node and a cutting taken at this point will root in soil or water. It must be firmly planted if it is to strike. Every grower should have a pot of spring cuttings so that there are youngsters ready both to give away and to replace the leggy veterans. Attention to culture, please, for the *tradescantia* is only attractive when at the top of its form.

## ZYGOCACTUS TRUNCATUS

Z.T., the Lobster or Crab Cactus, as it is known, is one of the favourite bracket plants in America because it can be relied upon to bloom about December 25th. It is an epiphyte growing on tree branches in its native land, Brazil.

It has rose-red fuchsia-like flowers that break out at the terminals of the leaves: the base of the petals are of a paler shade. The plant remains in flower for 6 weeks or more. The flat, notched and pendulous foliage is perhaps not very interesting, but the flowers that drip from the tips of the leaves more than make up for any dullness.

It looks particularly well when hanging from an orchid basket and appears to be most successful grown in this manner. An amateur has just reported that his basket plant, in a 5-inch pot has had 150 blooms. The orange and white hybrids are not so easy to buy.

*Culture*

Soil: 3 parts loam, 2 parts sharp river sand, 3 parts

▲ ZYGOCACTUS TRUNCATUS — *has rose-red fuschia-like flowers that break out at the terminals of the leaves.*

*Top left.* SAXIFRAGA SARMENTOSA — *this plant has roundish, reddish marbled leaves.*

◀ TRADESCANTIA — *known as the Travelling Sailor and Wandering Jew.*

thoroughly decomposed leafmould, 2 parts broken brick (about 1- to ¼-inch). Re-pot March.

The temperature must not be allowed to fall below 50°F. If the plant is to flower, it must have even warmth from September onwards. A place in a rather shady window, east or west, suits the Z.T. as it does not like the bright sunshine. If a south window is the only one available, the plant should be shaded. It is an easy grower that thrives in quite a warm room. While preparing to bud and in flower it should be left in a prominent light position and given a fortnightly dose of weak liquid manure.

After flowering, the plant may be moved into a more secluded, cool place — in the garden or on the windowsill if the weather is good, but beware of cold nights and heavy dews.

The watering-can may be used moderately until after flowering; then the plant should be once again kept on the dry side. From March onwards the plant will need scarcely any water, only enough to keep the foliage from shrivelling until the plant prepares to flower again.

*General warnings:* If the growth gets limp and flabby, the plant may have been overwatered. If the buds fall off, the cactus may be suffering from under or overwatering. Bud dropping can also result from draughts, fluctuations or gas fumes.

*Propagation:* by fronds cut with a razor from the parent plant in the spring or early summer and rooted in a sandy compost. The cuttings should be placed in a dry, airy place so that the cut surface can callus before planting.

ZEBRINA PENDULA — *a variety of tradescantia with dark mauve largish leaves.*

# PART THREE

A BAKER'S DOZEN FOR THE GRADUATE

# A BAKER'S DOZEN
# FOR THE GRADUATE

## BELOPERONE GUTTATA

The Shrimp Plant has always been a favourite of mine. I delight in its prawn-like flowers that appear in summer, and like its shrubby appearance and hairy leaves.

The shrimps or brownish-pink bracts that arrive on the terminal spikes are unusual and good lasters. The plant only flowers when mature and comfortably at home. The *beloperone* is a Mexican that grows to 2—3 feet; it has considerably less charm when out of flower, the leaves having a tendency to turn yellow and droop. This may be the result of too much or too little water or too cold a temperature. If the plant is cut right down in the autumn and the young shoots pinched back a couple of times the foliage will strengthen.

*Culture*

Soil: rich and retentive of moisture. John Innes No. 2. Particular attention should be paid to fast drainage. Pot in the spring. Likes the sun in a south window and moist warm conditions; it must never be allowed to dry out. Enjoys a moist pebble tray or to be packed in damp peat. Prune back in the autumn and place in a cool frost-proof place to rest until the spring.

*Propagation:* by trimmings when pruning or by young shoots, after flowering, in sandy compost.

## CITRUS MITIS (Calamondin Orange Tree)

This plant is closely related to the orange and comes from the Philippine Islands. It has sweet-smelling white flowers followed by small orange fruit.

*Culture*

This citrus requires a place on a sunny window-sill. It may take a little time to settle down in the house and drop a few leaves in the process. But fresh growth will come if the soil is kept moist but not soggy. A summer spray and an outing in the garden, the pot sunk in peat in some semi-shady spot, will be appreciated. A liquid feed may be given occasionally once the plant has settled in.

The *citrus mitis* is hardy, but an even temperature of 60°F. results in more flowers and fruit. J.I.P. No. 3 is a suitable compost; it may not be necessary to re-pot every year as the best performance is given when the plant is almost pot-bound.

*Propagation:* cuttings will root readily if kept close, and inserted in a sandy compost.

## EPIPHYLLUM

The Orchid Cactus, a shrubby species with large spectacular flowers and grotesque flat joints that are notched rather than spiny. The *epiphyllum* is a fantastically showy hybrid that comes in almost every colour except blue. One of the most brilliant house plants.

▶ CITRUS MITIS — *closely related to the orange and comes from the Philippine Islands.*

**E. ackermanii,** the popular red, is easy going while **E. cooperii** is white and sweet-scented, but not so regular in flowering. There are hundreds of stunning American hybrids, some more temperamental and delicate than others.

*Culture*

Soil: rich, porous, with a taste of cow manure; or J.I.C. No. 2. Pot in the late summer or early autumn after flowering and keep in a cool atmosphere and partial shade, but do not allow the temperature to fall below 45°F. The plant may be watered freely while growing but given less when resting, though the soil should never be allowed to dry out. Unlike the majority of its kind, it enjoys a spray with a syringe. In summer, give plenty of fresh air and put outside for a time. The *epiphyllum* responds generously to small doses of liquid manure, or weak doses of dried blood.

*Propagation:* by easily rooted cuttings or seeds.

## FATSHEDERA LIZEI

This is a fast-moving upright plant capable of growing to 8 feet or more: it is a cross between *Fatsia japonica* and the *hedera* (ivy) and its five-pointed leaves have an ivy look about them. Keep the plant bushy by pinching out the leader.

The variegated form, **F. l. variegatum,** is a delightful plant but *not* so easy (hence its place in the graduate's list). It is a slow grower and seldom rises above 3 feet. The broad cream-margined leaves make this a delightful solitary plant.

*Culture*

Soil: rich and leafy; or J.I.C. with an addition of beech mould. A warm temperature is appreciated. The variegated form needs a little more warmth and comfort and a good light without hot sun. It has no liking for central heating. The plant rests from October onwards when the water supply should be cut down, otherwise leaf dropping may follow, or the edges of the leaves turn brown.

*Propagation:* by cuttings. If the plant becomes leggy it can be beheaded and the top used as a cutting (see page 48). The parent plant will then break again.

◀ FUCHSIA 'EMILE DE WILDEMAN'— *an attractive almost hardy plant.*

▼ FATSHEDERA LIZEI — *a fast-moving upright plant capable of growing to 8 feet or more.*

## FICUS BENJAMINA

This is a delightful pendulous tree not unlike the birch with its pale bark. It possesses more grace than any other house plant I know. The long willow-like leaves have thin wisps at the ends that turn back like tails.

I should have placed this fig on the novice's list had it not been that mine had behaved so badly this winter shedding all its leaves. The plant is not easy if introduced to new surroundings during the winter (as mine was). Bought in the summer, it has time to reorient itself before the cold weather arrives. It requires an even temperature above 50°F. and if allowed to get too dry, it will wilt.

**F. lyrata** is another suitable fig for the graduate. Its leaves are fiddle shaped (waisted like a violin) and wavy edged; they are glossy and a fresh green. This plant likes steady conditions. It dislikes cold or heavily chlorinated water and is best kept fairly warm and under rather than over-potted. It will tolerate a darkish corner but not as a permanent place. (For *Ficus* culture see *F. elastica decora*, page 68).

## FUCHSIA

The fuchsia is an almost hardy house plant that deserves far more attention from the indoor gardener than it gets. There are a large number of attractive species available from the fuchsia specialists.

Those intending to make the Lady's Ear-drop their hobby plant (and I can think of none better) should join the British Fuchsia Society, which assists beginners, issues a journal and distributes plants.

Trailing fuchsias are perfect for hanging baskets.

▼ FUCHSIA 'CITATION' — *in early Spring this plant should be moved to a light position to get the morning sun and plenty of fresh air.*

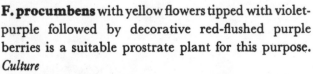

**F. procumbens** with yellow flowers tipped with violet-purple followed by decorative red-flushed purple berries is a suitable prostrate plant for this purpose.

*Culture*

Soil: leafmould, good loam and a sprinkling of sand or J.I.P. No. 2. Pot February to March. Temperature 40°—50°F. from late autumn into the winter. Some gardeners remove their plants to the cellar from October until February but any cool frost-proof place will do while the plant is resting. During this time it will require only just enough water to keep the wood healthy and the plant from drying out. About February, it can be moved into a temperature of 55°—60°F. and placed in a light position where it gets the morning sun and plenty of fresh air. This is the time for re-potting when necessary. Water sparingly until the plant is in active growth but spraying with tepid water both night and morning is helpful from February to May. Weak and straggling foliage may be pinched back as the plant develops. Protection must be given from the summer sun. Once the flower buds have formed, give weekly doses of mild liquid manure. Please do not move the pot around when the plant is in flower or you will risk bud-dropping. The flowering season ends in September, when water should be gradually withheld. Later the plant may be pruned back to the third or fourth bud before being removed once more to a cool place for the winter.

*Propagation:* the hardy varieties will strike during July and August; they should, when possible, be taken with a heel and must be given shade from the full sun. The half-ripe cuttings may be taken from the new

young shoots in March; they should be 4—5 inches in length. A long tumbler placed over the shoots will keep them 'close' and hasten development. The cuttings will grow through their first winter without a rest period.

## IMPATIENS

This perennial was so named because it was impatient in bursting its seed pod. As it spread from cottage to cottage, it gathered nicknames, among them Patient Lucy, Patience Plant or just Busy Lizzie. It is a relation of the garden balsam, with pink, red, mauve and white flowers.

*Impatiens* is summer flowering, but will flower through the autumn if seeds are sown in May or June or flower buds pinched back to defer the blooming period.

This is one of the easiest house plants to grow and I would have included it in the novice's list but for its vulnerability to virus disease (mosaic) and a tendency to fail during a severe winter if carelessly watered. It tolerates most things, even gas, while its gay flat flowers cover the bright green foliage.

Being an utter commoner, it has only during the last years been stocked by the nurseryman.

In the 18th and early 19th century, cuttings were handed from one gardener to another and a deserving strain was passed down from father to son and travelled the entire country. Now, on occasion, *impatiens* is promoted to the florist's window.

*Culture*

Soil: equal parts loam, leafmould, sharp sand chopped

small addition of pulverized limestone — John Innes No. 3 or any good rich, porous soil will do. Pot February or March. Sunny position in winter and partial shade during the hot summer months, when it must have constant watering, but the supply has to be cut down during the winter. Old plants are apt to grow leggy and should be rigorously pruned in the spring.

*Propagation:* by seeds and cuttings. The latter will strike at once during the spring or summer in sandy soil or water. The cuttings in water should be potted when well rooted and require more nourishment than water alone. Alternatively, a nutrient can be added to the water.

## MONSTERA DELICIOSA

This is a large impressive plant and can be recommended for a spacious room or studio. It comes from Mexico and is often known as the Hurricane or Swiss Cheese Plant because of the strange tears and holes in its leaves.

It is a willing grower and might have been included in the novice's collection, but I am anxious to see it better grown than is usually the case. If the handsome leaves are to be seen at their best, leathery, glossy and polished with possibly *three rows of holes or perforations* and sturdy aerials, the plant requires an even heat, humidity, good soil, plenty of root space and a gardener who knows his job. Seen at the top of its form it is quite a different plant to the specimen that is so familiar with dullish (and often dusty) leaves slashed only in occasional places.

None fits in better with steel furniture, zebra skins, oddities and modern decoration. In its tropical and native home, it is renowned as a bearer of fleshy, delicious and many flavoured fruits.

*Culture*

Rich light peat and leafmould compost or J.I.P. No. 2. A sprinkling of sand should be added. Pot early spring. Likes a warm, steady temperature if it is to grow; draught or cold will result in brown discoloration of foliage. Water freely in summer and moderately in winter, allowing the soil almost to dry out between waterings. The plant must be kept shapely; if necessary it may be decapitated and the top cutting planted in a sandy compost.

*Propagation:* by leaf and stem cuttings. The latter should be taken immediately below an aerial root.

When growing, tie aerial roots to the cane holding the plant, guide them towards the soil, and they will bury themselves.

## PEPEROMIA

The peppers are a tremendous family of about 500, many of which have attractively patterned foliage.

**P. caperata,** with corrugated leaf formation and small white flowers on slender spires, is the latest arrival.

**P. glabella** is a cream and green trailer that manages with a minimum of light and is often described as the radiator plant (it is certainly no lover of gas).

**P. hederaefolia** possesses rather charming pearl-grey ridged leaves but is a trifle tender.

**P. magnoliaefolia** has apple-green leaves bordered cream; a bright chubby little trough plant but slow growing. The variegated form and variety Green Gold are particularly attractive.

**P. sandersii** with silver-striped melon-shaped leaves on red-pink stems is the most popular member of the family but a little more difficult, as it does not like a temperature below 50°F.

These small plants are excellent for groups or baskets. The flowers are slender rat-tailed spikes, white or brownish and altogether unimpressive. Once *peperomia* has acclimatized, it is easy to manage.

*Culture*

Soil: a peat compost with plenty of sand and a lump of charcoal. Pot March. Likes moderate warmth, humidity and the moist pebble tray. The variegated foliage needs bright light without direct sun. Water moderately in summer and sparingly in winter, with tepid water; the plant is liable to rot if carelessly watered. If ring spot develops the leaves must be removed and burnt. The plant should be pinched back and kept shapely.

*Propagation:* by seed, or spring leaf or stem cuttings inserted in a moist peat-sand compost. Requires a little heat or the protection of a jam jar.

## PILEA

This house plant comes from the West Indies and tropical America.

**P. cardierei,** the Friendship Plant, is the most decorative of the family; a bushy dark green with red

*Left.* PEPEROMIA CAPERATA — *has a corrugated leaf formation and small white flowers on slender spires.*

tipped leaves and silver markings.

**P. nummularifolia,** or Creeping Charlie, with tiny round leaves makes a good hanging plant.

**P. microphylla,** or *muscosa*, is the dwarf of the family, mossy, plain and rather dull. The *pilea* is known as the artillery plant because the pollen from the flowers appears to explode as it is discharged. It is a dish-garden favourite and also useful as a colourful low grower in a trough. After watering, the leaves become luminous as if painted with aluminium.

*Culture*

Soil: rich and porous. J.I.C. No. 2 with an addition of peat and sand. Pot March. Likes a warm temperature, humidity and to be kept moist in summer by regular spraying, but has proved very hardy. Water less in the winter and do not wet the neat foliage. A fair

▶ PILEA CARDIEREI — *known as the 'Friendship Plant'. It has red tipped leaves with silver markings.*

light without sunshine is all that is required. The plant is allergic to gas, its leaves turning yellow then falling.

*Propagation:* by spring shoot cuttings inserted in moist sand.

## PRIMULA OBCONICA

A number of gardeners grow this primula with great success, their plants surviving for several years. Unfortunately, some gardeners cannot handle the plant without suffering a distressing skin trouble. The lilac, mauve-pink and purple umbels are delightful; the hairy ovate leaves, which are a pleasant green when the plant is at its best, are apt to get a trifle shabby during the resting season. The new large-flowered strains are to be had in superb clear colours and there are a number of charming hybrids to replace the pale mauves.

*Culture*

Soil: 1 part good fibrous loam, ½ part leafmould, dried cow manure and silver sand. Pot March or after flowering. The woodland primulas are always difficult to nurse through a hot summer and the best place for them is a north or west window as they need shade from the summer sun. Water freely and keep moist; desired temperature around 50°F. A fortnightly dose of liquid manure is beneficial before and during the flowering season. Dead heads should be removed at once otherwise the plant may stop blooming.

*Propagation:* by division after flowering and seed sown in May, which should whenever possible be raised under glass. Young primulas are free flowering.

## SCINDAPSUS

**S. aureus** has a striking appearance and is often mistaken for a variegated *Philodendron scandens* although its heart-shaped leaves are of a coarser texture. It is one of the best green and yellow (some call it lemon) climbers we have. It climbs or trails, but on the whole seems happier going up than down; it has not quite the vigour and pace of the philodendron. **S. marble queen** is a highly variegated form in white and green.

The foliage has a surprising characteristic: as the leaves progress along the stem, they increase in size. They have the reputation of being particularly vulnerable to rough treatment and bruising.

*Culture*

As for *Philodendron scandens* (see page 79). Variegation

improves if the plant is kept in a warm, even temperature, given a light position and protection from direct sunlight.

## SPARMANNIA AFRICANA

This is the lime's vigorous, quick-growing African cousin, an evergreen shrub with hairy, bright green leaves as much as 8 inches across. Known as the African Hemp, it is seen everywhere in Germany, where it is the much loved *Zimmerlinde*.

If happy in a room, the ends of the branches are decked in February or March with pleasant white flowers. The golden bunched red and yellow stamens are sensitive to touch; the feel of a finger or strange body makes them move aside. The *sparmannia* likes plenty of room, is quick growing and inclined to swamp its neighbours.

*Culture*

Soil: rich and porous; a compost of loam, peat and leafmould. Pot after flowering in March. If growing fast, the plant will require repotting several times during the spring and summer. However it will flower best if not overpotted. A fully grown plant is suitable for a tub. Feeds of a general fertilizer will assist its progress. Lowest winter temperature 45°F.; the plant is particularly vulnerable to draught, so should be placed in a good bright light, kept nicely shaped and cut right back if leggy.

*Propagation:* by springy cuttings that can be struck in water or sandy compost.

► *An attractive arrangement of indoor plants including* HEDERA GLACIER, HEDERA LUTZII *and* HEDERA ADAM; SAINTPAULIA CAVALIER, SAINTPAULIA DIANA PINK, GY-NURA SARMENTOSA *and* CYCLAMEN SILVER LEAF.

▼ *The arrangement in the right hand corner consists of* DRACAENA SANDERIANA, CYCLAMEN SILVER LEAF *and* SCINDAPSUS MARBLE QUEEN. *The arrangement at the back includes* BEGONIA REX, SCINDAPSUS MARBLE QUEEN *and* PHILODENDRON BURGUNDY.

◄ *An arrangement of indoor plants including* HEDERA CHICAGO, HEDERA CANARIENSIS *and* HEDERA CHICAGO VAR; PRIMULA, HYACINTH, FATSHEDERA LIZEI, CHLOROPHYTUM CAPENSE VARIAGATUM.

▼ IMPATIENS BALSAMINA — *one of the easiest house plants to grow, but has a vulnerability to virus disease and is apt to collapse during a severe winter if carelessly watered.*

# PART FOUR

TEN TEMPERAMENTALS FOR GREEN FINGERS

BRIEF NOTES ON OTHER PLANTS

# TEN TEMPERAMENTALS
# FOR GREEN FINGERS

## ANTHURIUM

This is the Flamingo, an aroid, and a member of the arum family: a spectacular flower with red, pink, yellow or white spathes and yellow tail-like spadix, flowering in winter or early spring. A large-leaved exotic and a demanding house plant that will test the gardener's quality.

For those who have never grown the plant before, choose **A. scherzerianum** from Costa Rica; it is far easier than its relatives. Standing less than 1 foot high, its fiery scarlet flowers appear quite frequently when the plant is satisfied with its surroundings. It has a selection of different-coloured spathes; these are among the longest-lasting flowers there are, the spathes remaining brilliant for two or three months. They are carried high on slender, elegant stalks.

The plants are sometimes grown for their foliage, but the flowers are the star-turn; the manner in which the spike straightens and the spathe turns down is spellbinding. The Flamingo is an arresting performer and many enthusiasts will wish to give the plant a trial.

*Culture*

Soil: equal parts loam, leafmould, sharp sand and chopped sphagnum moss. Potting time: January or after flowering.

This is a plant from the tropical forests that adores humidity and warmth. It must never be allowed to dry out. During the winter do not allow the temperature to drop below 55°F. The plants benefit by being packed in moist moss or stood on damp pebbles. A bright position should be chosen and the plant protected from the hot sun.

*Propagation:* by division of rhizomes at potting time.

## APHELANDRA

This is an extremely beautiful plant with flowers that arise from yellow, orange or scarlet bracts: the white-veined leaves are superb. Thoroughly worth growing for the foliage alone.

This is a capricious subject and until recently was looked upon as a stove plant. However, when I saw a splendid *aphelandra* that had been wintered in a flat by a novice, I began to think again. The plant stood on a sunny window-sill in a centrally-heated room; without central heating I doubt whether it would have been in such good order. I have seen plants die

▶ APHELANDRA LEOPOLDII — *a beautiful plant with superb white-veined leaves. This plant is worth growing for the foliage alone.*

off without notice even when in the hands of the most experienced of indoor gardeners.

**A. squarrosa louisae** has silver striped leaves and orange flower bracts, while a variety, **A. leopoldii** has a pale lemon inflorescence. The latter is a little temperamental about fumes and conditions.

The last addition to the family, **A. brockfield,** with yellow florescence, is shorter-jointed than its predecessors and tougher. Best of all, it has an erect habit and the leaves don't droop.

*Culture*

Soil: equal parts peat, loam, leafmould and sand. Potting time: March. Water freely in summer, moderately in winter, with tepid water. Never let the plant dry out. Ideal temperature: September to March 60°—65°F. A moist atmosphere is desirable; stand on a pebble tray or pack the pot in moss. Keep the plant in a bright light, protected from full sun: it may be cut back during February or March.

*Propagation:* by spring cuttings from side shoots in a heated frame or box.

## BEGONIA

Before dealing with the true house plants that belong to this family, something should be said about the two groups that can play a temporary role in our homes — the tuberous and fibrous-rooted begonias.

**Tuberous-Rooted**

Begin with good-grade tubers in March and start them in a shallow box, or pan. A suitable amount of peat should be soaked overnight in water and the

excess moisture squeezed out before using. A layer of
1—2 inches should be placed at the bottom of the
box or pan and the tuber lightly pressed, convex
side downwards, into the compost until it is lying just
above the level of the peat, with crown uncovered.
Plant lightly; the begonia cannot bear to be packed
down tight. If you are in doubt as to the top and
bottom of the tuber, place it on its side and wait for
growth to start.

The box can now be put on a shelf in a dark, warm
place, watered sparingly and the tubers coaxed into
growth. The ideal temperature is around 65°F. but
anything over 50°F. will do.

After a few days, pips and roots will appear when
more light can be given but not strong midday sunlight. Should buds form, they must be removed. The

▲ BEGONIA

▲ BEGONIA SEMPERFLORENS

tubers must be kept moist but not soggy, or they will rot.

When well rooted, the pips will open to leaves about 1-inch across and the plants should be moved first into 3½-inch pots and, when 3-inches high, into 5-inch pots. J.I.P. No. 1 with an addition of peat and a sprinkling of sand should be used with light fingers.

Whenever the top soil looks dry, water generously allowing any surplus to drain away. Good results are to be had by standing the pot on pebbles in a dish of water, but the base of the pot must be held above the water by the pebbles.

The begonia enjoys an occasional weak feed with Liquinure during the growing season. If big flowers are wanted, pinch out the two outside buds.

After flowering, gradually cut down the water

supply and, in late autumn, place the pot on its side in a dark place until the crown has dried off; a week or two later the soil can be shaken away. The tuber should then be examined for decay, any rot cut out and the wound dusted with powdered charcoal. The tuber can then be stored for the winter in a frost-proof place where the temperature is not above 50°F. otherwise it will dry up and shrivel.

Hot days, followed by cold nights often result in bud dropping. Also heavy begonia heads have a habit of falling off just when they have reached their zenith. This means that either too much or too little water has been given.

Not only the size but the price of the tuberous begonia has increased exceedingly. But beautiful plants, sold under coloured headings, pink, red, yellow, orange, and white, are to be had at a reasonable cost.

## Fibrous Rooted

**B. semperflorens** The small fibrous-rooted bedding begonia makes a charming house plant for months on end. I always advise lifting a few from outside beds before the frost destroys them. After potting, they should be placed on a sunny window-sill where they will flower unchecked by the move. The new improved hybrid strain Thousand Wonders, white, rose and red, blooms profusely. Water well and feed regularly.

## Rhizomatous

Now to the Rex begonias and some of the favourite house plants, the painted-leaf begonias with marbled, banded or spotted leaves of wine red and silver, and grey purple and green. They are carried on hairy stalks and are entrancingly patterned. The flowers are often dull and should be removed so that all effort may go into the foliage.

Filagree, sometimes known as Hélène Teupel, is hard to beat. The jagged leaf is dark green, blotched silver and purple, with a metallic sheen. Turnford Hall and others might well be from the tropics.

The gardener should go for those with compact habit and not too large a leaf and remember that begonia rex should be allowed to remain in the same pot until it becomes almost pot-bound. In all circumstances, wait to re-pot until late spring.

**B. boweri** This has lately come into fashion. Only a few inches high, this creeper has small bright green leaves, maroon-edged and delicate white flowers. It is inclined to be fussy, so water carefully.

*Culture*

The begonia likes a porous soil, a compost of 2 parts

▲ BEGONIA METALLICA — *has ribbed, hairy olive-green leaves with a metallic sheen and light pink flowers on short stalks. This plant is easy-going, provided the temperature does not fall below 50°F.*

loam, 2 parts peat, 1½ parts leafmould and 1 part sand. The plush leaves are vulnerable to dust and quick to curl up in a stuffy room. The plants are almost dormant during the winter but must not be allowed to become bone dry. Wait until the pot is full of roots before repotting; the pot-bound live longer. Give the plant semi-shade in the summer and beware of wet leaves scorching in the sun. The winter temperature should not be allowed to fall below 50°F., avoid a dry, hot atmosphere by providing as much humidity as possible.

The begonia has a horror of gas.

### B. Rex Leaf Cuttings

This is an excellent and fascinating way of propagating. The chosen leaf should be large, unblemished and cut off with a complete stiff stalk. A shallow seed pan should then be filled with fine compost of a high sand content, which has been passed through a sieve. The stalk stem should then be firmly inserted up to the point where the leaf and stem join, permitting the leaf to lie flat on the soil. Four notches should be made at points where the heavy veins radiate from the leading vein. The leaf may be pegged with hairpins or kept in place with pebbles; stability of position is important.

The pan containing the leaf should be covered with glass and kept close; the glass should be wiped over and turned when moist. Rising sap will form a callus at the places where the leaf has been notched, roots will grow there and finally tiny plants will appear.

This is not an easy operation without heat, but is worth attempting. Leaf cuttings are best taken in the summer.

### Some of the more tractable begonias

**B. haageana**  Large pale green leaves and clusters of pink shell-pink flowers — some quite deep in colour, arriving intermittently throughout the year. Those attracted to this plant should grow *haageana* hybrid Papa de Chevalier.

**B. glaucophylla**  A perfect pendulous plant with shiny pointed leaves that droop gracefully from delicate stems, and red-brick flowers. It will not tolerate hot rooms, relying as it does on humidity.

**B. maculata**  The thick dark-green leaves are spotted white and there are inconspicuous pale pink flowers that come and go almost unnoticed.

**B. masoniana**  First known as the Iron Cross, with grey-green leaves bearing a purple cross. I have found this decorative plant difficult to grow: it needs a steady warmth of 60°F. throughout the winter.

▶ ANTHURIUM SCHERZERIANUM — *a plant from Costa Rica which is far easier to grow than its relatives. It has a selection of different coloured spathes carried high on slender, elegant stalks.*

**B. mazae**  A small plant with maroon-plum coloured leaves, red undersides, and pale pink flowers on long stalks. Once acclimatized this plant becomes amenable.

**B. metallica**  Ribbed, hairy olive-green leaves with a metallic sheen, and light pink flowers on short stalks. Easy-going, provided the temperature does not fall below 50°F.

**B. serratifolia**  Finely divided reddish leaves spotted pink with pink spring and summer flowers in loose racemes.

### Three hybrids of interest:

**B. abel carrière**  Silver heart-shaped leaves: red flowers emerge from the leaf axils.

**B. corolicta**  A tall grower with white dots on the light green leaves, and small racemes of red flowers.

**B. president carnot**  Tall and strong, grows to 6 ft. or more. The scarlet flowers are produced generously in the conservatory but only occasionally in the house.

## BROMELIADS

This is a large Central and South American family that includes a host of unusual plants adapted for drought, desert and neglect. Many of them are of rosette formation with stiff, hard and ornamental leaves of arresting colours: lime green, red, shocking pink, brown, silver and grey, blotched and banded and sometimes translucent. A number are epiphytic air-pines, perching themselves on another plant, handy roof or telegraph pole. In some cases the leaves are closely packed together, forming a watertight bottle or leaf-vase in the centre. Water poured into

► *An arrangement of indoor plants consisting of* BEGONIA REX, CYCLAMEN SILVER LEAF *and* SAINTPAULIA DIANA BLUE.

◄ *The arrangement in the right of the picture consists of assorted* BROMELIADS *and* SCINDAPSUS MARBLE QUEEN. *In the left of the picture there is an arrangement of* SANSEVIERIA TRIFASCIATA LAURENTII, RHOICISSUS RHOMBOIDEA JUBILEE, HEDERA CANARIENSIS *and* ARALIA SIEBOLDII VARIAGATA.

▼ *Below: an arrangement of assorted* CRYPTHANTHUS, *members of the bromeliad family. This family includes a host of unusual plants adapted for drought, desert and neglect. Many of them are of rosette formation with stiff ornamental leaves of arresting colours. In some cases the leaves are closely packed together, forming a watertight bottle or leaf-vase in the centre.*

this flask will be slowly absorbed.

The rosettes produce only one inflorescence (flowers composed of bracts that are modified leaves); when its descendent offsets are rooted, it dies. The gardener will be left with one or several offsets, which he may detach and plant in a sandy compost or the plant may be left in its pot and the dead rosette cut out. The young offsets will not flower for a couple of years or more. I may say it is a triumph to flower a plant without artificial heat.

Americans use the plant's leaf-vase for daffodils, lily of the valley and others. This is disgraceful behaviour destroying the dignity of a lovely shaped plant.

The nomenclature of the family is still being sorted out, but it is safe to buy a *bromeliad* as they are all dramatic and desirable.

### Aechmea

The most popular member of this genus, *A. rhodocyanea*, received the Royal Horticultural Society's Award of Merit in 1959. The large rosette of grey-green leaves with white and silver stripes is impressive, while the central leaf vase or cup is always of interest. From this comes the spike that carries the lavender blue flowers and pink bracts. The florist usually offers the plant when the long-lasting florescence has begun to open. The soil must be kept moist while the plant is in bud and flower.

**A. fulgens** has dark green leaves with maroon undersides. The flowers are purple-blue in loose formation and surrounded by flame-red berry-like sepals.

### Billbergia

A genus, named ofter the Swedish botanist J.G. Billberg, that is a native of Brazil and Mexico.

**B. nutans** is probably the best known of the group. Easy and almost hardy, *B. nutans* is spectacular when in flower. The pendulous bloom of blue, yellow and green is a veritable horticultural rainbow but, once it fades, the plant with its dullish, sedge-like leaves becomes insignificant.

### Cryptanthus

This is a favourite hobby plant in America where it is known as the Chameleon (the leaves change colour when moved in and out of the sun). The plant is of rosette formation (without a vase or cup) and the leaves stiff with crinkled edges.

The white flowers are unimportant but the plant's star-like appearance adds glamour to a group arrangement.

**C. bivittatus** has pink and white stripes on its flattish rosettes in a striking star-fish pattern.

**C. tricolour** is pale cream and becomes suffused with pink if given a bright enough position.

**C. zonatus** possesses broad, long and stiff leaves with transverse stripes and has white flowers.

### Neoregelia and Nidularium

Both species come from Brazil; they have rather insignificant pale-lilac flowers that appear for 24 hours or so in the plant's cup or funnel. These should be picked off with tweezers when faded and the cup washed out; otherwise there is likely to be an unpleasant smell.

**Neoregelia spectabilis,** the Painted Fingernail, has a red ink thumb-mark on the tip of each leaf.

**Nidularium tricolor** has flat rosettes, narrow white and green pointed leaves and a blue-red centre.

### Vriesia

**V. splendens** sometimes known as Painted Feathers, is tolerant of low temperatures (down to 45°F.) and dark corners. The soft green leaves are banded while the undersides are a pleasant maroon.

*Vriesias* seldom flower until 7—8 years old. Afterwards offshoots appear in the rosettes and these flower in their turn during the next year or two. Removing the offsets and rooting them is a difficult operation.

The gardener must not be surprised if his *Vriesia* dies away once the plant has flowered, for this can happen. The yellow inflorescence of sheath bracts will last for weeks, but the flowers themselves fade at the end of a day.

**V. carinata** is particularly handy for filling in a

plant arrangement.

A soil of ⅓ pine needles *(Pinus sylvestria)*; ⅓ leaf mould (oak or birch preferable to beech); ⅓ peat. All quantities by volume.

Many *Bromeliads* stay happy in the same pot for years. When re-potting becomes necessary, do it in the spring, and efficient crocking is essential. The plants should be watered freely in summer and sparingly in winter. Fill the leaf-vase or funnel with rain or boiled water at room temperature. Hard water is apt to mark the leaves. This plant enjoys humidity and an occasional spray. Given the right potting compost, extra feeding is not required. Put in a semi-shaded position during a hot summer.

Winter temperature should not be allowed to fall below 55°—60°F.

*Propagation:* by large offsets preferably in heat (80°F. for speed). In the case of the *Aechmea*, leave on the parent plant, the latter being cut away from the root with the sharpest of knives once the florescence has lost its glory.

As to the rest of the family, all sideshoots should be severed low, with a fraction of root attached whenever possible.

## CYCLAMEN

The Persian Violet from Asia Minor is one of the most beautiful winter flowers, a tuberous-rooted perennial with white, pink and red flowers.

In the hands of novice gardeners they seldom survive long in the house, the plant needing more humidity than that of the ordinary living-room. It resents dry atmospheres and hot places, preferring a steady temperature of about 45°—50°F.

A steady temperature of 60°F. during the day, falling some 10°F. at night is sufficient once the plant is acclimatized. The earlier in the autumn the plant is bought, the better its chance of getting used to its surroundings before the fires are stoked high.

### Culture

Study the reference to humidity (see page 15) and do all possible to provide the desired extra moisture in the air. Moist peat-packing is always appreciated. Water generously during the flowering period and give weak doses of liquid manure every other week; water at the side of the pot, well away from the corm. Faded flowers and dead leaves can be given a slight tug and removed from their sockets. If portions of

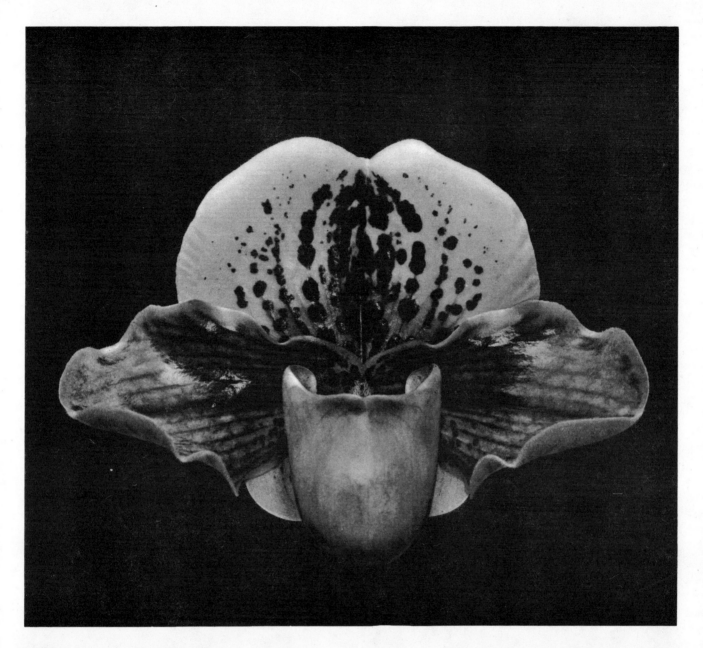

stem are left, they may set up decay.

Cyclamen thrives in an east window with plenty of light and good ventilation; it needs protection from the full sun and is particularly sensitive to draught. On no account must it be placed close to a fire.

After flowering, when the leaves have turned colour and died down, the tired top soil and dead foliage should be removed and the pot laid on its side in a cool frost-proof place. Water may be given very occasionally, to keep the corm plump and in good condition. Some gardeners put their plants in a shady spot in the garden during the summer.

Re-pot in August. Soil: 2 parts loam, 1 part leaf-mould and 1 part sand with a final sprinkling of sharp sand and bonemeal. The fleshy corm should peep out above the surface soil; some prefer to set the corm half in and half out of the soil. Shallow planting is essential, otherwise moisture will settle in the depression at the crown of the corm and cause decay. For this reason it can be watered from the bottom of the plant, thus avoiding any danger of water stagnation and rot.

The cyclamen should be under-potted as the almost pot-bound condition encourages free flowering. Water should be given sparingly until active growth is begun, but care must be taken that the plant does not dry out.

The cyclamen is capable of dying without warning or suddenly collapsing but those who enjoy succeeding with the capricious will enjoy growing it.

### CYPRIPEDIUM

The orchid is not an easy house plant, but is by no

means as temperamental as is generally supposed. There are cheaper as well as expensive species and the Amateur Orchid Growers' Society will provide advice about culture and buying. It is wise to buy a mature plant from a reputable firm.

The *cypripedium*, the Lady's Slipper or Moccasin Flower, brown, yellow and green with a mass of speckles, should be the novice's first orchid. This wax flower, with the protruding lower slipper-petal, arrives in the winter and lasts for weeks on end. It is getting cheaper and should soon be within the reach of everyone.

*Culture*

Soil: equal parts fibrous peat, chopped sphagnum moss to which broken pieces of charcoal may be added. Fill ⅓ pot with crocks to ensure fast drainage. Re-pot after flowering or in March or April and, whenever possible, seek the assistance of an orchid grower as re-potting orchids is tricky. If a plant is not uncomfortably cramped, it can stay put for 2—3 years. When potting, space should be left for a final top surface of sphagnum moss.

Hanging teak baskets make excellent containers and should be put in partial shade, or a pot can be placed on a tray or saucer of moist pebbles and left in a north-east or north-west window. The *cypripedium* must be protected against hot sun and gas fumes.

Water lightly until the plant has settled down. When growing, it can be sprayed and watered freely, as it loves humidity. Keep a uniform moisture throughout the pot and allow the soil to dry out between waterings. Foliage should be sponged and kept clean.

Fresh air in moderation, a warm room with a winter temperature around 60°—65°F. are basic needs.

*Propagation:* by most careful division at potting time.

## HIPPEASTRUM *(amaryllis)*

The Belladonna Lily or Knight's Star is a bulbous plant often known as amaryllis. The flower may be pink, red, purple, cream-white or candy-striped, with 3—5 heads on a majestic stalk. Appearing in spring or summer, it is a flower of spectacular beauty. It has improved both in size and colour during the last years but the bulbs remain expensive. However, large-flowering seedlings from selected stock are usually to be had at a reasonable price and these give long-lasting blooms of immense size for years.

▲ MARANTA TENCONENRA.

*Left.* MARANTA — *a very beautiful foliage plant.*

*Culture*

Soil: 2 parts turfy loam, 1 part sharp sand and a sprinkling of bonemeal or addition of crushed bones, of John Innes No. 3. Potting may be done in the winter. Prepared bulbs planted in November will flower at Christmas time. The pot should be 1—2 inches larger than the bulb. A 5-inch pot will usually suffice. In a large pot the bulb concentrates on root-making at the expense of flowering. Over-potting and deep planting are responsible for many disappointments. Bulbs must be planted with at least two-thirds of their surface above soil level.

Plunging is of great benefit to the amaryllis or it will root satisfactorily in a dark cupboard in 6—8 weeks. Water should be applied sparingly until the flower buds appear, after which it may be freely given. Light syringing and fortnightly doses of liquid manure are helpful.

After flowering the plant should be left in a sunny position and, if the gardener takes care of the strong strap-like leaves until they die back, he will be rewarded by handsome flowers the following year. Feeding should continue until the leaves turn yellow.

This plant enjoys the summer plunged in the shady border until there is danger of frost and will benefit if treated to mild doses of Liquinure until the leaves die back. When the foliage is brown and loose it should be removed and the pot stored in a dark, cool place where the temperature does not fall below 60°F. From now on, while resting, the bulb will need only enough water to keep the soil from drying out.

Re-pot just before the plant starts into growth, using the same or a slightly larger pot. As the *hippeastrum* dislikes disturbance, the soil can be scraped away and the plant top-dressed.

*Propagation:* by bulblets that form close to the base of the parent bulb, which can be removed at potting time. Wait until they come away willingly; if they possess a root structure, so much the better.

The Lily of the Palace will be worth the trouble even if it flowers only two years out of three. It is certainly the Emperor of indoor bulbous plants.

## MARANTA

The small *maranta* is a very beautiful foliage plant. **M. leuconeura** is a low-growing dwarf, 6—8 inches high; its velvety leaves are a fresh green with maroon-purple diamond markings.

Since this plant closes its leaves at night or almost curls them together, it is known as the Prayer Plant, or Husband and Wife plant. The habit is the plant's protection against the heavy tropical dew in its native lands.

**M. massangeana,** the Fishbone Plant, small and flat-growing (about 2 inches high) is striking and gorgeous in colour: green, silver, purple and brown with pale veining. The ornamental foliage is fascinating; the white flower is insignificant. **M. zebrina** is also elegantly veined.

I have put this jungle plant on my third list only because it is so slow and loathes to acclimatize to room life, constantly hankering for the heat and humidity of the greenhouse.

As a matter of interest, **M. arundinacea** provides arrowroot and tapioca.

*Culture*

Soil: J.I.C. No. 2, plus a small amount of peat and sand. Pot in March, keeping the soil light and porous. Good drainage and shallow pots are important. A warm temperature, a position out of the draught and partial shade are essentials. Syringe frequently when the atmosphere is dry and provide as much humidity as possible. The water supply should be cut down from September onwards, as the plant rests from November to February.

*Propagation:* the tuberous roots can be divided in spring. Offshoots can also be taken in March and struck under cover of a glass jar or, better still, in heat. Stock is best kept young.

## PLATYCERIUM ALCICORNE

The Stag's-horn fern from Australia deserves a boost. It has only to be better known (and better advertised) to become the rage among ferns; fitting in with modern decor, it is the ideal plant for the surrealist gardener.

The *platycerium* is an epiphyte (not a parasite), attaching itself and clinging to other trees. These striking long indented leaves, flaring out and shaped like reindeer's antlers, are ready to flatten themselves against any friendly branch or trunk. At the base of the plant is an altogether different kind of leaf that shades the roots, catches any debris that afterwards provides soil and assists the antlers in their work. The showy fronds are grey-green; the dustbin leaf turns brown and more or less camouflages itself out of sight.

I have included this interesting plant in the green-finger list, because it requires a skilful hand to accommodate it comfortably, so that the fronds may embrace and grip some suitable surface, as in their native land.

A wooden base wrapped with osmunda fibre, held in place with copper wire, should be provided. The fern seems happier like this than potted or in any basket arrangement. Cork bark is always appreciated if roots are packed round with peat fibre.

*Culture*

Soil for potting: 2 parts fibrous peat, 1 part turfy loam, 1 part equal proportions of charcoal, broken pots and sand. Potting time: February to March. The fern should only be re-planted when necessary. Temperature: October to April 40°—50°F.: May to September 50°—65°F. A light and airy position should be found where the plant can hang; it should be given protection from the summer sun and possibly moved into a shadier place. But there should be only one move during the year as this subject dislikes motivation. Water moderately all the year round. An occasional spray or dip in the sink will be welcomed (but not in the winter). The prostrate primary leaves turn brown but must not be removed nor fronds sponged. Young plants are fussier than adults.

*Propagation:* by side shoots in the summer, under glass. Temperature: 55°—60°F.; shade must be given.

## SAINTPAULIA *or African violet*

'The *saintpaulia* likes the Americans,' a New York

*Top right.* AECHMEA RHODOCYANEA — *has a large rosette of grey-green leaves with white and silver stripes. The spike which carries the lavendar blue flowers comes from the central leaf vase.*

◀ PLATYCERIUM ALCICORNE — *has long indented leaves, flaring out and shaped like reindeer's antlers.*

▶ SAINTPAULIA *or* AFRICAN VIOLET — *comes from the tropics and enjoys the moderate steady warmth of central heating.*

grower told me. It is true that it grows well in their warm rooms for the little plant demands an exacting gardener and the right conditions; but it likes the English too. Meanwhile its dislike of cold or uneven temperatures and draughts has led to thousands of mouldy demises.

## Temperature

The plant comes from the tropics. It is not a violet but claims a relationship with the gloxinia; it enjoys the moderate steady warmth of central heating. The *saintpaulia* will tolerate an unheated room provided the temperature does not fall below 60°F. during the day and 50° at night; a further fall and the foliage will curl under and gas fumes are actively resented.

Move your plant away from the window-sill on a cold night. Ventilation without draughts is essential.

## Light

The *saintpaulia* must have light and will not bloom generously in a sunless north window; it basks in the morning sun but must be protected from full sunshine. It favours fluorescent lighting (see Artificial Light, page 14).

## Humidity

Humidity has to be provided if the plant is to thrive. The moist pebble tray, the damp moss top dressing, moist peat packing, constant syringing and the occasional steam bath (see Humidity, page 15) are all aids and a steaming kitchen kettle will also help.

## Soil

The compost should be porous enough to hold moisture and light, so that the roots can travel easily. Leafmould, well soaked before using, horticultural peat and sand make a suitable mixture. John Innes Compost No. 3 is often used. Some gardeners enrich it with a small quantity of beech leafmould. A sprinkling of powdered charcoal helps to keep the soil sweet.

## Watering

Water in the early morning in summer and at midday during the winter; it is important that the plant should be dried out by evening. The temperature of the water should be warmer, rather than colder, than that of the room; cold water is responsible for leaf spot and icy water can kill. Hard water is apt to mark leaves so rain water is always preferable. Use a thin spout and keep the water away from the crown of the plant. Wet crowns result in the stems turning brown and stem-rot. It is difficult not to lose a few leaves in this way: if smitten, dust the stems with flowers of sulphur. Water from bottom or top as preferred.

▶ *This picture shows a* BEGONIA MASONIANA — *first known as the iron cross. It has grey-green leaves bearing a purple cross.*

*Far right:* HYACINTHS *bulbs should be planted a pencil width apart and should have their noses visible above soil level.*

*Below right: The four plants shown in this picture are varieties of* SAINTPAULIAS *or* AFRICAN VIOLETS — *Diana blue, pink and red.*

To water from the bottom, fill a saucer 1 inch deep and allow the plant to absorb as much as it needs. After a short while, any excess water should be tipped away. Some gardeners wick water (see page 30) with success, others water top and bottom alternately, so keeping the moisture uniform throughout.

## Feeding

Weak doses of any well-balanced fertilizer are helpful, particularly before flowering time.

## Resting Period

A plant will at times stand still, but the *saintpaulia* appears to have no regular resting period.

## Potting

Underpot rather than overpot: re-potting time is the moment to divide plants; single crowns are, in my view, preferable to multiple ones and shallow pots are desirable. Generally speaking, plants are best grown with one crown, the embryo crowns being removed once large enough to handle.

## Buying

Plants can be bought at shops and nurseries; there are also *saintpaulia* specialists. Plantlets (small plants) are available, but unrooted leaves, usually a minimum of 6, are considered a good way of starting a collection. Personally, I think the beginner should start with a rooted plant.

Single blue Cordelia and the deep blue Flying Dutchman are particularly good beginner's plants. Skyway, Pink Geneva, Blue Boy and Stukey's Triumph are also on the easy side. Englert's Blue Diana and Pink and Red of the same name, are good growers. The dark leaves are better doers than the pale green varietites, being more resistant to rot. Pink

◄ LILIUM AURATUM — *makes a superb pot plant. It should be grown in a cool greenhouse and brought into a cool, airy room when in bud. A moist atmosphere is essential at all times.*

▼ REBUTIA — *small spiny globose cacti which flower freely from the base in a large range of colours.*

Rococo is the best double pink up to date and White Pride and Double Delight are good. Wrap moist newspaper round the pots to provide moisture and camouflage this with green moss.

## Propagation

*Seed* Requires a temperature of 75°–80°F. to germinate.

*Leaf* Each leaf may produce as many as 12 young plants. The stem should be cleanly cut with a sharp knife and then planted upright in a well-crocked seed pan. Vermiculite (see page 23) or peat with a generous dollop of sand may be used as a starting medium. The leaf can be propped up with small sticks if inclined to wilt and tumble. Keep the pan in a warm temperature, or a propagating case (see page 48) and immerse it from time to time from the bottom in tepid water. Do not wait for it to dry out before taking action.

If you haven't a propagating case, a jam jar or tumbler will do. This must be lifted once a day and kept clear of moisture. The breath of air will benefit the leaf.

After 5 weeks, the leaves should have sent out roots, but wait until the sixth week before potting them. Use a rich porous compost and light fingers. In a couple of weeks a cluster of leaves will present themselves and, when these become plantlets large enough to handle, they may be parted from the leaf and re-potted. Do not throw away the mother leaf as it may be used in the same manner several times.

## Rooting Leaves in Water

A jam jar should be filled with rain or distilled water, a lump of charcoal added, then the jar covered with waxed paper held in place with a rubber band. A hole is then pierced through the paper and the stem of the leaf passed through so that it reaches the water. The jar should be placed in a warm position out of the sun. When the plantlets appear, they can be removed and potted. If the leaf flops, it should be carefully planted in soil.

## Flowering Period

As a result of unfortunate publicity and sometimes overkeen salesmanship, the novice has been led to believe that the *saintpaulia* never stops flowering. The fact that it has no fixed month or months for flowering has also led to misleading statements. It is fair to say that it is a very free flowerer when happy but, along with other plants, it enjoys and takes a rest when it feels like it. So long as it looks healthy, this is in order.

## Varieties

There are the singles and doubles; the latter have the reputation of being a trifle shy in flowering. Supremes, miniatures, climbers and trailers are on their way here from the States.

## Winding Up

A little understanding of the *saintpaulia* will go a long way. Novices and veterans are advised to join the Saintpaulia Society.

There are two 'musts' — a warm room and an attentive gardener.

# BRIEF NOTES ON OTHER PLANTS

**ABUTILON.** Erect, can be treated as semi-climbing shrub. Green and variegated bell-shaped flowers: red, pink, orange, yellow and white. Sun. Winter: 50°—55°F. Re-pot spring. *Propagation:* cuttings spring and summer.

**ACHIMENE.** Tuberous-rooted summer stove plant (sometimes known as the 'hot-water' plant): violet and mixed hybrids of velvet texture; best raised in a greenhouse, will consent to live indoors. Rhizomes should be planted ½-inch deep in shallow boxes of moist sand and leaf-mould, January to March: later pot up in compost of 2 parts peat and loam, 1 part leafmould and sand: give occasional mild doses of liquid manure. Support floppy shoots with twigs. Keep dry after flowering and, before winter, remove and store rhizomes in dry sand in temperature of 50°F. *Propagation:* by division of tubers in February: cuttings of young shoots April.

**ADIANTUM.** Maidenhair fern. Moist atmosphere essential. Spray and provide humidity. Dislikes: towns, draught, dry air, full sun, central heating, gas and cigars. *Propagation:* division best; spores on moist sandy peat under glass.

**AGAVE.** Century Plant; succulent. Easy. Many get too big; small striped species such as **A. victoriae-reginae** advised. Sun lovers. Protection from frost. *Propagation:* offsets.

**AMPELOPSIS HETEROPHYLLA.** Virginia creeper; variegated climbing deciduous plant; green and red foliage. Winter: light frost-proof place. Prune spring. Good light: shade

midday sun. *Propagation:* cuttings with two buds or layering.

**ARALIA.** See **Dizygotheca.**

**BOUGAINVILLEA.** The glabra variety with magenta flowers is sometimes grown as a house plant. Climbing shrub. Gay bracts. Sun-lover. Rich soil: bonemeal. Under-pot. Hot summer: garden. Winter: warm and dry indoors. *Propagation:* spring cuttings; ripe shoots and root cuttings.

**CACTUS**

**Aporocactus flagelliformis.** Rat's tail cacti. Red flowers, rather insignificant. Long flexible tails ½-inch thick. Good basket plant. Rich humus soil. Keep out of hot sun. *Propagation:* cuttings.

**Mammillaria.** Pincushion, ribless and generally globular. Over 250 members of the family. Many flower easily. Small but charming. Taste of lime in soil. Semi-shade. Winter: dry. *Propagation:* seed and cuttings.

**Opuntia.** Prickly pear or Bunny Ears. Flattened or cylindrical shoots. Flowers red, orange or yellow. Limey porous soil. Easy. *Propagation:* joints (that often fall off).

**Rebutia.** Small spiny globose plants; flower freely from base, in large range of colours. Easy. Novice should grow rebutians and pass on to mamillarias. *Propagation:* seed and cuttings.

**CALADIUM.** Stove plant with superb arrowhead leaves, sometimes almost transparent. Height

ABUTILON — *a semi-climbing shrub with bell-shaped flowers.*

120

1—1½ ft. **C. candidum** has white leaves edged with green and green veins; Lord Derby is translucent rose. Tubers started in March to April in temperature of 80°—85°F. Compost of equal parts turfy loam, peat, leafmould, decayed manure and silver sand. Even temperature around 65°F. desirable: moist atmosphere essential. Shade, not summer sunshine. Leaves, sometimes almost transparent.

**CAMELLIA.** Shrub. Shiny foliage. Flowers single, double, pink, red or white. Garden summer. Spray: keep moist, and cool. Draughts, dryness or cold cause bud dropping. Pot August. Fastidious. *Propagation:* spring cuttings.

**CAMPANULA ISOPHYLLA.** Perennial; pale mauve flowers or small white bells: imperturbably hardy when established. 6-inches high. Ordinary good soil: enjoys a summer period in the garden.

**CODIAEUM.** Croton: shrubby plant: sunset-coloured foliage: red, yellow and green. Curious shapes, flat and corkscrew. Tender, heat lovers, *difficult* house plants. Leaf droppers. Many dislikes: draught, cold, dryness, full sun. Likes: rich soil, generous watering when thirsty. *Propagation:* early spring cuttings in heat.

**COLUMNEA.** Hanging basket plant: happier in greenhouse than room. Temperature 60° to 70°F. Soil: equal parts fibrous peat, sphagnum moss and charcoal. Repot March. *Propagation:* cuttings 3-inch firm shoots in heat.

**CYPERUS ALTERNIFOLIUS.** Umbrella plant: grass-like leaves: stiff stems: fluffy flowers in centre coronet. Warm room, semi-shade, rich, sandy soil: swamp lover, enjoys a little water in the saucer. *Propagation:* by leaf rosettes or division.

**DIEFFENBACHIA.** Dumb Cane or Mother-in-law Plant (leaf under tongue said to bring silence). Large oblong leaves spotted or patterned. Heat and moisture, spraying, partial shade and rich leafmould soil. Grows to several feet, but lower leaves apt to die off. Fortunately the plant makes new leaves at the top more rapidly than it loses the bottom ones.

Likes central heating; temperature must not be allowed to drop below 50°F. Difficult and poisonous. *Propagation:* cuttings in heat.

▲ ARALIA ELEGANTISSIMA — *has a dark mauve feathery foliage with finger-like leaflets.*

*Top left.* ADIANTUM CUNEATUM — *variety of the adiantum.*

◀ ADIANTUM — *this fern requires a moist atmosphere. It dislikes draughts, dry air, full sun and central heating.*

**DIPLANDENIA.** Stove plant seldom happy in a room. Beautiful mauve flower. Temperature: steady 55°—60°F. Prune October. Soil: rough fibry-peat with ¼ silver sand. *Propagation:* spring cuttings 3-ins. in sandy peat under bell glass.

**DIZYGOTHECA (ARALIA) ELEGANTISSIMA.** Dark mauve feathery foliage with finger-like leaflets. Likes central heating, moist atmosphere and feeding. Water carefully winter. *Propagation:* cuttings; spring and summer in heat.

**DRACAENA (CORDYLINE) TERMINALIS:** (Dragon Plant). A family that must have warmth and humidity.

**D. deremensis warnecki** — grey-green leaves with silver stripes.

**D. firebrand** — narrow pink and red leaves.

**ECHEVERIA.** Mexican succulent. **E. carnicolor** forms fleshy rosettes of bluish green. Orange-red bell flowers. Sun. Winter 50°—55°F.: away from fire. Re-pot after flowering; leafmould, sand and mortar rubble. A recent arrival at the florists. *Propagation:* small leaves root at once.

**EUCALYPTUS GLOBULUS.** Blue Gum tree: glaucous rounded leaves. Gum exudes from bark. Easily raised from seed. Cool, humid conditions and constant 'potting on'. Usually too big after one year. Sun, rich soil and feeding. Hot summer: garden. *Propagation:* seed; January, February or August.

**EUONYMUS.** Japanese Spindle tree. Shrubby. Several variegated forms. Yellow and white markings. Tolerates dry heat. Keep nicely shaped. *Propagation:* softwood cuttings spring and summer.

**EUPHORBIA SPLENDENS.** Crown of Thorns: small red flowers, prickly stem. J.I.P. with sprinkling of sharp sand: good light, plenty of warmth: minimum winter temperature: 50°F. Keep fairly dry in winter, prune May. *Propagation:* early summer cuttings: dry out for 2 days before insertion.

**FATSIA JAPONICA.** Often known as Castor Oil Plant. Dark green multi-lobed leaves. Cool, partial shade, rich soil, generous watering. *Propagation:* seed and hardwood cuttings.

**FITTONIA.** Low-growing shiny oval leaves, white veins. Shade. Light porous soil. Difficult to

*Right.* ▶ MAMMILLARIA WILDII — *variety of the mammillaria which needs a little lime in soil and dryness during the winter.*

*Below left.* APOROCACTUS FLAGELLIFORMIS — *known as the Rat's tail cactus. It has long flexible tails - ½inch thick.*

*Below right.* OPUNTIA — *variety of cactus with flattened or cylindrical shoots.*

*Left.* MAMMILLARIA — *a cactus generally globular in shape.*

*Top right.* REBUTIA — *small spiny plants which flower freely from the base, in a large range of colours.*

*Centre right.* REBUTIA SPINOSISSIMA — *variety of Rebutia.*

*Lower right.* BOUGAINVILLEA GLABRA — *a climbing shrub with magenta flowers. It needs sun and a rich soil.*

supply warmth and humidity needed. Draughts
and careless watering kill. *Propagation:* cuttings in heat.

**GLORIOSA SUPERBA.** The orange and red
Malabar lily. A dramatic summer flowering
climber that should be brought into the house
when in bud. Culture: compost of equal parts
loam, peat, leafmould, decayed manure and
silver sand. Pot February, placing one tuber
2-inches deep in a 6-inch pot or several in an
8—12-inch pot. Water sparingly until plant
begins to grow, then freely. After flowering
withhold water and keep soil dry until
February. Winter temperature 55°—65°F.
*Propagation:* by offsets removed when repotting.

**GREVILLEA ROBUSTA.** Silky Oak. Tree: silver
fine-cut fern-like leaves. Likes cool, but tolerates central heating. Loves sun but tolerates
semi-shade. Must not be allowed to dry out.
*Propagation:* seed or top cutting (plant becomes
leggy).

**GYNURA SARMENTOSA.** A delightful purple-
tinted foliage plant that has grown well for me.
The florist has found the velvet nettle sensitive
to shop conditions and therefore, takes an un-
favourable view. The orange and insignificant
flowers are best cut off near the main leaves of
the plant as soon as they appear. Plant enjoys
mild central heating, good light: allow to dry
out between waterings. Beware over-watering.
Repot March. Soil: equal parts peat, loam,
leaf-mould and sand: Prune: spring. *Propagation:* spring cuttings.

**HOSTA (FUNKIA)** Japanese Day Lily: herbaceous lilac flowering. **F. variegata,** white
splashed leaves. Good loam; well-rotted manure. Plant ½-inch deep, ½-inch apart, 5-inch
pot. Pot: October—March. *Propagation:* division.

**HOYA CARNOSA.** Quick-growing climber. Fleshy
leaves in pairs. Clusters of white waxy flowers.
Semi-shade. Foliage marks in sun. Likes plenty
ventilation. Summer: garden. Do not cut dead
flowers or next year's bloom will be lost.
*Propagation:* spring cuttings.

**HYPOCYRTA GLABRA.** A thick-leaved trailer
with orange-scarlet heather-like flowers in
pairs at leaf axils. Good wall subject for bright
position. Must be encouraged to take winter
rest, otherwise, will not flower. Not hardy.

◀ CAMPANULA ISOPHYLLA — *a perennial with pale mauve leaves or small white bells, which likes a spell in the garden.*

*Centre left.* ECHEVERIA — *a Mexican succulent.*

*Lower left.* DIPLANDENIA — *this plant has a beautiful mauve flower.*

▼ EUPHORBIA SPLENDENS — *also known as Crown of Thorns. It has small red flowers and a prickly stem.*

▼ FITTONIA — *this plant has low-growing, shiny oval leaves with white veins.*

*Propagation:* tip cuttings spring.

**IPOMAEA.** Morning Glory, one of the loveliest of climbing half-hardy annuals. Best bought as a seedling raised under glass. The enormous saucer-shaped flowers of Heavenly Blue are superior to the striped Flying Saucers and new-comers. Enjoys sun and prefers climbing a stable cane to a swinging string. *Propagation:* by seed sown ⅛-inch deep in pots. Temperature 65°F. March.

**IXORA FULGENS.** Small shrub: dark green foliage: clusters of white, pink or orange tubular flowers. Heat and moisture essential. Keep dry after flowering. Rich porous soil and feeding. *Propagation:* cuttings in heat.

**KALANCHOE.** Succulents, fleshy with red and orange flowers. **K. tomentosa** silvery, furry; reddish leaf-tips great charm. Sun-lover. Light porous soil. Under-pot. **K. blossfeldiana,** scarlet flowers, florist's plant. *Propagation:* seed sown in heat, March summer cuttings of un-flowered shoots.

**LACHENALIA.** The Cape Cowslip, greenhouse bulbous flowering plant that can be brought into the house before flowering. Compost of 2 parts fibrous sandy loam, ½ part leafmould, ½ part decayed manure and sprinkling of coarse sand. Pot August ½-inch deep. Temperature 45°—55°F. Dry off after flowering and rest June to September. *Propagation:* by offsets at potting time.

**NEPETA GLECHOMA VARIEGATA.** pretty basket plant. Leaves silvery, trailing. Easy. *Propagation:* division roots or by cuttings: October – March.

**NERTERA DEPRESSA.** the Bead Plant: with small leaves, orange berries. Prefers cool green-house to room conditions. Shady position. Soil: rich sandy loam and leafmould. *Propagation:* seed in heat, or division of rooted stems, spring.

**OXALIS.** (Oxalidaceae 'Wood Sorrel' Shamrock). Herbaceous perennial. Much grown in North. Warm window. Sandy loam. Pot August. Water moderately until leaves appear: then freely. *Propagation:* division roots or offsets.

**PALM.** The army of uncared-for palms seen in hotel lobbies are bereft of tropical appeal. Palms manage without sun but cannot do themselves justice without light. Keep slightly pot-bound, top dress in spring, feed water sparingly in winter. Minimum winter temperature 50°F. Soil: 1 part leafmould, 3 parts fibrous loam, 1 part coarse sand and a little cow manure and bonemeal. *Propagation:* side shoots.

**Chamaerops humilis.** Fan-leaved. Easy.

**Cocos weddelliana.** Coconut palm, feathery, short-lived.

**Howea (syn. Kèntia).** Flat, slender leaves: pendulous.

**H. belmoreana** slower, more erect, hardier, more elegant than **H. forsteriana.** Both grow from one stem; satisfactory house plants.

**Neanthe bella** from Mexico, small, good semi-shade loving. Surprising rather than attractive flower.

**PANDANUS.** Screw-pine. Narrow re-curving green- and-white striped leaves; palm-like. Steady winter warmth essential. **P. caricosus** small tree, charming; fountain-like slim leaves, white flowers. Soil: leafy loam. *Propagation:* suckers in heat.

**PASSIFLORA.** Passion flower. Temperate house conditions required for flowering. Foliage decorative.

**P. caerulea** hardy; leaves apt to shrivel winter.

**P. edulis** one of best indoors. Soil: rich. Water freely when growing. Prune during winter rest. *Propagation:* seed, cuttings, layers.

**PLECTRANTHUS.** Ideal edging or for troughs: 2—3-inches high. Fleshy, heart-shaped, pink-veined leaves.

**P.oertandahlii** dark purple undersides. Soil: peaty. *Propagation:* cuttings in heat.

**PLEOMELE REFLEXA VARIEGATA.** Song of India from Ceylon. Leaves beautifully margined by wide bands of golden yellow or cream, arching and graceful; slow grower and rather delicate. Soil: 2 parts screened beech mould; 1 part horticultural peat; ½ part coarse sand, 4 oz. John Innes Base Fertiliser. *Propagation:* cuttings of growing tips spring.

**SCHEFFLERA ACTINOPHYLLA.** Leaves divided into five glossy leaflets (mature plants). A New Zealand introduction: slightly tender: flowers in panicles at leaf axils. Easy: ordinary fare. *Propagation:* seed.

**SELAGINELLA.** Creeping moss. Soil: equal parts fibrous peat and chopped sphagnum moss. Potting time February—March. Water copiously April—September and syringe. Shade, warmth and moisture. *Propagation:* autumn cuttings.

**SENECIO MACROGLOSSUS.** Vigorous climber. Relation of common groundsel with a waxy leaf, gold markings and a distinct look of the ivy. A real plant that looks artificial. Soil: medium to heavy loam. Should be fed generously during growing season. *Propagation:* spring cuttings February to August.

**SONERILA MARGARITACEA.** Stems and leaves with red glow: pink flowers early spring. Prune hard after flowering to encourage fresh growth: warm, moist conditions: temperature not below 60°F., otherwise leaves will fall. Shade

◀ GREVILLEA ROBUSTA — *has silver fine-cut fern-like leaves.*

from direct sunlight. *Propagation:* cuttings in heat January—May, seed.

**SPATHIPHYLLUM WALLISII.** Akin to miniature white *anthurium* requiring similar fare (see page 98). Hood-like spathe, opens green, turns white, then back to green: long lasting. Highly glossed leaves: veining gives ribbed effect: shade to avoid bleachint. Greedy.

**S. MONA LOA** is a similar but a larger and more impressive plant. Greedy. Re-pot June: feed well: steady winter temperature: minimum 60°F. and humidity essential for happiness. Water moderately winter. *Propagation:* by division.

**SUCCULENTS.** Many already mentioned. Excellent house plants sunny room; south window.

▶ HOYA CARNOSA — *a quick-growing climber which has clusters of white waxy flowers.*

Dry air, winter 40°—50°F., only enough water to prevent complete dry-out and shrivelling. From house-leek to Lithop (Living stone): individual and interesting. *Propagation:* cuttings; seeds.

**SYNGONIUM.** Emerald Velvet. Erect and creeping: aerial shoots: dark-green leaves triangular with pale green zones along mid-rib. Light red spathes. Tolerant. Soil: J.I.P. with ⅛ total bulk extra peat. *Propagation:* tip cuttings rooted in pure peat: small propagating box: humidity required, 70°F.

**TETRASTIGMA OR VITIS.** Rampant five-fingered leaved climber. Fast grower; over-watering may cause top shoot to drop. Rich soil: large pot. Greedy feeder. Winter: almost dry. *Propagation:* cuttings; bottom heat; not easy.

**THUNBERGIA ALATA.** Black-eyed Susan, a climber that has gay orange-coloured flowers with black centres. White and buff varieties also desirable. Best grown indoors as an annual. Enjoys the sun and seems to prefer to climb short canes than to hang. Benefits by feeding when in bloom. *Propagation:* by seed in heat, February to March.

**TOLMIEA MENZIESII** pick-a-back plant. Heart shaped, hairy, light green leaves. Young plants arrive on lower leaves. Easy. Soil: ordinary. *Propagation:* plantlets on leaves will root as they reach the soil. Can be raised from seed sown indoors or garden in March or April.

**ZANTEDESCHIA AETHIOPICA (Richardia africana).** Arum Lily or Lily of the Nile. White-spathed. Superb. Winter. Tubers, singly in 6-inch pots, with neck of tuber showing. Plant August—September. Feed liquid manure before flowering. Rests summer: plunge outside. Light: not direct sun. *Propagation:* seed, cultivation small suckers (tubers).

## HANDY REFERENCE LIST FOR PARTICULAR CONDITIONS

**Flowering Plants**

| | |
|---|---|
| Fuchsia | Pelargonium |
| Impatiens | Saintpaulia |
| Kalanchoe | Sparmannia african |

**'Toughies'**

| | |
|---|---|
| Aspidistra | Philodendron |
| Ficus decora | Sansevieria |
| Hederas | Tradescantia |
| Helxine | |

**For centrally-heated rooms**

| | |
|---|---|
| Aechmea fasciata | Crotons |
| Bilbergia nutans | Ficus benjamina |
| Cacti | Platycerium alcicor |
| Cissus antarctica | |

**For sunny rooms**

| | |
|---|---|
| Beloperone guttata | Impatiens |
| Fatshedera lizei | Monstera deliciosa |
| Hederas | Pelargonium |

**For shady positions**

| | |
|---|---|
| Ficus pumila | Philodendron |
| Helxine | Scindapsus |
| Maranta | Tradescantia |

# PART FIVE

# SPRING BULBS

Bulbs are not, of course, true house plants. However, I think it may be useful if I press home a few important points that lead to their success if grown indoors by the house plant gardener.

- Buy from a reputable bulbsman and order in good time in the early autumn.
- If choosing early hyacinths, tulips or daffodils, keep bowl to one variety.
- If your bowl has no drainage holes, use fibre with charcoal.
- Soil must be fresh and sweet.
- Bulbs are easier to manage if planted a pencil width apart.

**Depth** Hyacinths and daffodils should have their noses visible above soil level, but tulips should be covered (and the small bulbs too).

The best way of rooting spring bulbs is to plunge them (burying the pots or bowls) in a shady place, cover with soil to a depth of several inches and leave for 8—10 weeks. The bulb can then make good root formation before developing top growth.

The dark well-ventilated cupboard is another method. Some gardeners grow their bulbs under the bed with considerable success.

When the bulbs have made 1—2 inches' growth, bring them *gradually* into the light.

**Watering** At no time allow them to dry out but avoid sogginess.

If the novice finds that he has overwatered, drain away the overflow by tilting the bowl to one side.

Rain water is ideal. Very cold water should not be used.

**Placing** It is vital to keep bulbs near the light. The window-sill is the best place. They should be kept the room-side of the curtain at night.

Bulbs will last longer if kept out of the full sun when in bloom and moved from a hot centrally heated room at night.

**After flowering** The bulbs grown in fibre will be utterly exhausted. Those grown in soil will have given much of their strength; it is expecting too much of a house-grown bulb to flower again with the same vigour the second year. The ideal plan is to pass the bulbs on to a country gardener, who will find a quiet corner where they can regain vitality, then to buy afresh.

Whatever the plan, the leaves must be given time to die down and return their nourishment to the bulb's store cupboard. Premature cutting or removal of foliage is disastrous. Attention to small details is important.

▶ MUSCARI ARMENIACUM *(grape hyacinth)* — *when planting hyacinth bulbs, their noses should be visible above soil level.*

*Below left.* SINGLE NIVALIS *(snowdrop).*

*Below right.* DOUBLE NIVALIS *(snowdrop).*

*Lower right.* NARCISSI CANTATRICE — *the best way to root spring bulbs is to bury the pots or bowls in a shady place, cover with soil to a depth of several inches and leave for 8—10 weeks.*

*Lower left.* DAFFODIL — *when planting these bulbs, keep their noses above soil level.*

# THE FLORIST OR GIFT PLANT

The plant that comes straight from the greenhouse via the florist finds conditions indoors hard, if not intolerable. These are *not* house plants but merely temporary residents, accustomed to everything of the best, including controlled even heat and tropical humidity. Arriving at the peak of their splendour, they resent the sudden change of atmosphere, the new, abrupt or often timid gardener lacking the professional etiquette with the can.

Many of these plants die before they have finished flowering, lasting little longer than a bunch of tulips or daffodils. Placed in a draught or on top of the fire, they pass out in a matter of hours. Some nursing homes dump the patients' plants in a draughty corridor for the night; here the azalea and begonia suffer, while the cineraria collapses in the early hours of the morning.

A gift plant will last longer if it is kept out of the draught and away from the fire. Never let it dry out completely and provide as much humidity as possible. This can be done by standing the plant on a pebble tray or packing the pot in moist peat or moss; pebbles and moss must be kept slightly damp. It is distressing when a plant in bud declines before its bloom and beauty are spent. There are some plants that have nothing more to give once they have flowered and can be thrown away as blooms fade.

hardy perennial that is forced for spring and Easter bloom. Some of the new hybrids, including America lilac-rose, Gladstone white, Queen Alexandra pink, and Red Sentinel, flower freely with tightly packed bunches of small flowers along the stem; the foliage is light and fern-like. This is a thirsty subject; one of the few that does not mind being overwatered. After flowering the plant should when possible, be returned to the garden border and another brought in during the spring or dug up from the garden early the following year. It should be started in a cool room, 45° to 50°F., and later transferred to a warmer room, 55°—50°F. It likes a bright window, peat soil or J.I.P. No. 1, and when in bud and flowering, several wettings a day. Propagation is by division in the autumn.

## Azalea indica

The Indian azalea is a native of Japan; it is a showy plant, white, pink and crimson, and comes from the humid glasshouse, for which it never ceases to hanker. Many of these plants arrive from Belgium and Holland, where the nurseryman pinches out the lateral shoots, which means that the plant will not bloom

## INDIVIDUAL PLANTS

### Astilbe

The spiraea or false Goat's Beard from Japan is a

▶ AZALEA INDICA *and other Christmas pot plants. The* AZALEA INDICA *is a native of Japan and requires frequent watering.*

the following year.

This is the most popular birthday, anniversary and invalid gift plant of the winter. The florist should tell the client to regard the azalea as a temporary guest only. If the owner can keep his plant handsome with the leaves healthy and intact until after flowering he has done well. It should be kept moist, and away from fire and radiator.

The azalea is usually pot-bound and therefore thirsty; it should be watered freely and is one of the few that may be watered from the bottom. If placed on a tray of moist pebbles, frequently syringed, and extra humidity provided it will keep its leaves and last far longer (see Humidity, page 15). The plant will benefit by being taken out of a hot room at night and put in a cooler place out of the draught.

After flowering I advise the gardener to give his plant to a friend with a greenhouse where it will take a year or so to recover from its experience in the house.

If you decide to keep your azalea, remove all dead heads after flowering and cut down the watering, never letting the soil dry out completely. Put the pot in a cool, light frost-proof place until the second week in May and then plunge it in its pot in a shady place in the border. Water regularly and watch for the red spider. An occasional dose of liquid fertilizer will be appreciated (chemical fertilizers should be avoided). In September, dig up the pot and top-dress or re-pot as necessary with acid peat, replunge as before in the garden, leaving it until the end of October. Once back in the house, prune the dead wood and hope for the best. If the azalea flowers again, even in a half-hearted manner, you are to be congratulated.

## Begonia

Gloire de Lorraine is popular and, at its zenith, a mass of small pink-lace bloom. It must be kept warm, moist and out of the draught. Looked after, it will last for three weeks or longer, when it may be discarded.
**Bulbs** (see page 132).

## Calceolaria

The spotted slipper plant is an annual; it should be kept moist and will last longer if moved out of the full summer sun. It dislikes heat and should be kept as cool as possible.

## Cineraria

Here are the large-flowered *stellata multiflora* and the double varieties with daisy-like florets. This plant has a long autumn and winter season and the heavy trusses are in every brilliant colour other than yellow. It dislikes hot and stuffy rooms and full sun, and is particularly vulnerable to draught. The soil must be kept moist; if allowed to dry out, the plant wilts and seldom recovers. Once the flowers are over, the *cineraria* has served its purpose.

## Coleus

The ornamental nettle from Java is a decorative florist's plant and, with its velvet and many-coloured foliage, makes a first-rate bedder but not altogether successful house plant. It is difficult, if not impossible to winter in a room as the plant needs a warm, light place. Lack of light will result in the leaves losing their beauty, then dropping. Pinch out the points of the shoots to keep the plant bushy and remove the insignificant flowers when they appear The coleus may be fed weekly, and should be kept moist. Cuttings root easily in soil or water. Keep young stock coming along in case the parent plant disappoints you. J.I.P. No. 1 or equal parts of leafmould, loam and sand suit the coleus. Beware of the mealy bug (see page 54).

## Erica

The good-luck heathers from the florist and heaths, originally from South Africa. Grown by specialists in a greenhouse, they find it difficult to settle down indoors, so are not amenable as permanent house plants. However, if you wish to try to save a plant, keep it cool and water normally with rain or soft water, for it is a lime-hater. Stand the plant in the garden from June to October and re-pot in the spring, using a peaty soil.

## Euphorbia pulcherrima: Poinsettia

This beautiful Mexican that flowers at Christmas time with vivid scarlet bracts is difficult to keep in

▲ ERICA HYEMALIS — *this plant finds it difficult to settle indoors. Stand the pot in the garden from June to October and re-pot in the spring, using a peaty soil.*

▼ EUPHORBIA PULCHERRIMA *(Poinsettia) — flowers at Christmas time with vivid scarlet bracts.*

the house after it has flowered. It is deciduous. Sunshine and an equable temperature of 60°—70°F. are essentials, gas fumes are fatal. It prefers a south window and a stationary position. Cut down the water supply gradually when the bracts fade and keep the plant slightly dry until May. Then prune and re-pot if necessary, in a sandy loam with an addition of peat. The plant can now be watered moderately and plunged outdoors until September.

**E. fulgens** has arching stems and flowers surrounded by brilliant orange bracts.

The new cream-yellow Paul Mikkelsen hybrids are a welcome addition to the family. It is hoped they will withstand temperature changes rather better and last longer than their predecessors.

### Exacum affine

This is a free-flowering biennial, first introduced to this country in 1848 but only now establishing itself at the florists. It is lilac-blue, fragrant and will flower for months in partial shade. It can be wintered in a temperature of 60°F. and re-potted or top-dressed in the spring with fibrous loam and sand. Grows easily and is reasonably cheap.

### Genista

A greenhouse plant and a member of the broom family with delightful fragrant golden blossom. It is never a happy house plant; it requires sun and a warm, steady atmosphere and if the plant is kept in good order until the pea-shaped blossom is over, the gardener has done well.

### Gesneria

A red, tuberous-rooted perennial with pea-shaped summer flowers. First introduced in 1752, it went out of fashion, but now has returned. It likes a warm, light room, normal watering and weak doses of liquid manure when in bud and flower. If keeping the plant, gradually reduce the water after flowering and stop feeding. Rest the plant in a cool, frost-proof place and keep it dry. Re-pot in March with a good compost. Propagation by increase of tubers, cuttings in peat, or detached mature leaves

### Gloxinia

This tuberous-rooted perennial is more at home in the greenhouse than a room, so put it in a warm spot out of the full sun and keep the soil moist. Water from the bottom to spare the beauty of the downy leaves. Re-pot January to March in equal parts of fibrous loam, fibrous peat and leafmould with an addition of well-decayed manure and a sprinkling of silver sand. The astonishingly rich and glorious flowers, require artificial heat. They will not grow at their best in a room.

## Hydrangea

The heavenly blue hydrangea that arrives from the florist about Easter has been severely forced so it may last only for a couple of months. It will be very exhausted by the forcing treatment and may need up to 2 years before it returns to health and normality (flowering in July as Nature intended).

It is better to start with an unforced plant, bought flowering in the early summer. Besides blue and pink, there are now lavender, violet and crimson varieties.

*Culture*

The hydrangea thrives on a soil of 2 parts rich loam, 1 part peat and 1 part well-decayd manure and a sprinkling of sharp sand. It should be potted and pruned after flowering, the flower-bearing and weak wood removed. Next year's flowers come from shoots of the previous year's growth, so be careful. If it can be put in the garden in some shady spot for a while, so much the better and the outside window-sill is the next best thing. The hydrangea requires plenty of water when growing; this means a drink once or twice a day and, when very dry, a soak in a bucket of water. From January until March scarcely any is needed.

In September transfer the plant to a dark cellar or a cool place until January, when it may be returned to a sunny position. Later protect it from the hot sun or it will flop.

The blue hydrangea depends much for its colour on an acid soil, so do not allow it to come in contact with lime. Special colouring powder can either be mixed with the soil when potting up or used as a top dressing and watered in. The blueing powder which is generally available, must not be allowed to come in direct contact with plant roots. 3 ounces of aluminium sulphate added to 1 gallon water is another solution that will help to intensify the colour of the blues.

*Propagation:* by stem cuttings (young shoots) taken in March or April under glass or, better still, inserted in a propagating box.

## Lily

The lily makes a superb pot plant. It should be grown in a cool greenhouse and brought into a cool, airy room when in bud. A moist atmosphere at all times is essential.

Pot November to March, using a compost of ⅔ fibrous loam, ⅓ well decayed leafmould and a good sprinkling of coarse sand and a few lumps of charcoal.

▲ EXACUM AFFINE — *a free-flowering biennial. It has lilac blue, fragrant flowers, which will bloom for months in partial shade.*

▼ GENISTA — *a member of the broom family with delightful fragrant golden blossom.*

139

Pot firmly, only just covering the top of the bulb and add more compost as stem roots appear. Plunge in the garden (facing north, or cover with 6—8 inches of peat fibre. When growth reaches 1 inch, remove to greenhouse or to a window in a cool room. Water sparingly at first. Top dress stem roots as they appear. Good ventilation and fast drainage is essential. Liquid manure is welcome once a week while plants are in full growth.

After flowering, remove seed pods, leaving stem and foliage undisturbed and place pots in a cool and shady place. Continue watering until plants show signs of dying down, which ends the growing cycle. Watering should then be withheld.

*Propagation:* by offsets at potting time (not an undertaking for a beginner).

## Marguerite

The Paris Daisy with its gay white flowers and blue leaves will last three weeks in a room if kept moist and given ordinary care.

## Primula

The primula is a delightful greenhouse plant. *P. kewensis* has fragrant, deep yellow flowers. *P. malacoides* mauve to purple blooms, while *P. obconica* is to be had in rose, blue, red, white and salmon, but is responsible on occasion for skin trouble to which certain gardeners are allergic. *P. sinensis* has velvet leaves and attractive pink, lilac and white flowers.

The primula becomes shabby-looking after a long stretch in the house and the foliage yellows.

## Rose

The little China rose does not make a good perma-

nent house plant so is in the florist or gift-plant group.

The small bushes, with stems of no more than 9 inches, will flower from May until October when in good health. Their generosity in flowering puts the hybrid teas to shame. But their life is limited to 6 months or so if not given at least 18 inches of soil, outside conditions, clean air and refreshing rain. So treat your rose as a temporary house guest.

Among the most stalwart of the group are Baby Crimson, flame and gold Baby Masquerade, shell-pink Cinderella, bright-red Granadina, scarlet-crimson Red Imp and the veteran rose-pink Roulettii. Unfortunately, few miniatures as yet are sweet-scented.

### Solanum pseudo-capsicum

This is the Jerusalem or Christmas Cherry, native of Madeira, with bright scarlet winter berries. *S. capsi-*

*castrum* has conical berries in purple, red or white, and there are a number of hybrid strains. These plants are perennials but better results will usually be had by buying afresh each year. If kept, they should be given a cool, light position, plenty of water and occasional doses of mild fertilizer. Daily misting is one of the secrets of success. Once the berries have fallen, the plant should be pruned back hard and repotted in a rich soil; underpotting usually encourages flowering. Now place your plant in a cool position or plunge it in the garden until September. Do not put into a hot room, in dry atmosphere or with a gas fire.

The florist's plant has an important place in this book, because many gardeners like to save their gift plant whatever its performance. I hope I have assisted their endeavour.

◄ GLOXINIA — *has downy leaves and rich and glorious flowers.*

*Right.* PRIMULA OBCONICA — *a delightful greenhouse plant which can have rose, blue, red, white or salmon flowers.*

*Lower right.* SOLANUM CAPSICASTRUM — *these plants are perennials and have purple, red or white berries.*

▼ LILIUM REGALE — *makes a superb pot plant.*

# MINIATURE TREES

An oak, chestnut and many other trees can be grown on the window-sill. All they need is air, moisture and light. The acorn may be started in a special glass or the neck of a bottle where its germination can be watched. I raised my first oak in a decapitated egg-shell. A young spreading chestnut has tremendous charm and can be moved from pot to tub, but all young saplings in their contrasting greens are a delight

## DWARFS

Small dwarf trees — cedars, cypress, spruce and pines — will live indoors if given enough light and summer airings on the window-sill. They can be obtained from nurserymen who specialize in miniature and sink gardens.

## BONSAI, THE JAPANESE METHOD OF STUNTING

The Japanese have done this for some 2,000 years and their skill is world famous, but this method is still comparatively new to most of us. A fir stunted by a master hand will be well under 12 inches; its shape, habit and line will follow exactly that of its full-sized counterpart. The gnarled trunk, the rather tortured yet superbly balanced branches and the weather-beaten appearance are a work of art. The Japanese is only satisfied with the perfect replica.

The cunning is not to be mastered in a day, but we are beginning to learn the rudiments.

The first requirement is a small seedling of 6—8 inches. An oak, birch, beech, sycamore, maple, cherry, willow, chestnut, plum or crab-apple will do and may be found in a garden, wood or orchard. If time is no object, it can be grown from seed and a suitable container chosen.

A small shallow earthenware pan, a cream carton, half a grapefruit or orange skin will suit the purpose. I prefer the carton or fruit skin as the roots can be cut back when they penetrate the container, while the tree in the pot or pan has to be turned out. The carton should be pierced in a number of places for the roots to make their way through.

The tree should be planted in a fibrous loam, leaf-mould or any compost in early spring and put in a light, cool place.

There is nothing further to be done during the first year, other than to keep the seedling healthy, which may entail daily watering.

By the second year, the roots should be poking through the carton or skin. They should be snipped off with sharp scissors. If the seedling is in a pot, it must be carefully knocked out and the main roots trimmed.

▶ BONSAI TREE — JUNIPERUS CHINENSIS VAR. SARGENTII — *45—50 years old.*

142

The top growth will now require twisting and training with copper wire, sticks or trellis. There are no rules, but any surplus strong growth must be cut out and branches tied down when sap is rising. Neat hands and the Japanese highly developed sense of line and composition, plus their gift for imitation are needed. The second year is vital, a good start being all-important.

From now cn the little tree should be re-potted every spring until it reaches the desired height and dimensions and always fitted into the smallest container possible. The tree should, at this stage, depend entirely on fibrous roots.

If at any time it should flag or hesitate, sprinkle with steamed boneflour to induce courage and confidence. At no time should the sapling be allowed to dry out or toast in the hot summer sun.

Although the major part of the training is carried out during the first three or four years, the tree must be constantly watched and trained for a long time to come. Fresh air and unremitting care will count for much.

▲ MINIATURE TREE — PINUS PENTAPHYLLA — *this tree has been stunted by bonsai, the Japanese method of stunting. The skill of the Japanese is world famous, but their method is still comparatively new to us. A fir stunted by a master hand will be well under 12 inches, its shape, habit and line will follow exactly that of its full sized counterpart.*

◄ MINIATURE FIR TREE — *the cigarette in the picture gives an idea of the size of the tree.*

# FRUITS

I am in favour of growing fruit and vegetables in the house, particularly in the nursery. In my early youth, the fruit stone that had been on my plate, even in my mouth, had something intimate, personal and very endearing about it. I was a passionate fruit grower with a treasured pineapple plant, orange and lemon trees and a date palm. The success of these plants was due to their being planted moist in warm if tired nursery soil. I was, I remember, a generous waterer.

## PINEAPPLE

The plant's silvery re-curving long-toothed foliage is distinctive; the leaves grow to four or five feet in their native land. The crown (a nice fleshy disc) should be sliced off at the top of the fruit and is best planted in a sandy compost. I grew mine in a saucer with a little water, where it seemed to thrive for an eternity. But looking back I suspect the life of my pine was but a few months.

This is a member of the bromeliad family (see page 104). Pot on as the plant becomes root-bound. Good light and sun are essential; minimum winter temperature 65°F.

## AVOCADO

The avocado has come into its own during the last few years and the large seed can often be seen perched on three matches (or happier still toothpicks) in a widemouthed jar. Its base should touch the water in the manner of a hyacinth in a bulb glass.

The seed should be soaked in warm water before being suspended and the outer covering removed.

Care must be taken to hang the seed with the small end up, and to see that the water supply is replenished as it evaporates.

When the seed splits, the glossy-leaved tree can be seen arriving; this is fascinating. Soil may now be added to the water so that the transition from water to soil is gradual and easy. The avocado can equally well be grown in a 4-inch pot, planted ½-inch deep in a sandy compost. Every now and then a seed will rot: this is just bad luck and not the gardener's fault.

Trouble may arise when the plant becomes too big to be accommodated in the house. I tried to find a home for a handsome specimen grown by a reader, but in vain.

## ORANGE, LEMON, GRAPEFRUIT AND TANGERINE

Most of us can obtain seeds or pips from these fruits during the course of the year. Washed and planted, 3 to a pot in a moist sandy soil, they make delightful small trees with particularly attractive shiny foliage. The tangerine will be found to be extra glossy.

Keep the pots warm and shaded until sprouting takes place, then move the plants gradually to the window-sill. During the warm summer months they should be put outside, so that the wood can ripen.

## DATE

To grow a date-palm, plant at least 4 stones, as some may prove infertile, in a sandy compost and cover over with a glass sheet to help germination. The seedlings should be kept in an oven-warm heat until the narrow leaves mature.

▲ PINEAPPLE — to grow pineapple, remove a fleshy slice from the top of the fruit.

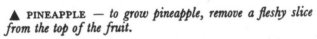

◀ ANANAS COMOSUS — a pineapple as a pot plant.

Top right. PINEAPPLE — filling the pot with sandy compost.

Centre right. PINEAPPLE — when the pineapple has been planted, press the soil firmly with the fingertips.

Lower right. GRAPEFRUIT — grown from pips or seeds they make delightful small trees.

Lower left. ORANGES AND ORANGE BLOSSOM — small orange trees can be grown from seeds or pips from the fruit. They should be planted three to a pot in a moist, sandy soil. When sprouting takes place move the plants gradually to the window-sill. The orange tree has a particularly attractive shiny foliage.

# VEGETABLES

Fond as I am of fruit trees, I am equally enthusiastic about nursery verdure. A plant that seems to me to be sadly neglected is the sweet potato. It is reliable, rapid and even dashing, which is exactly to the budding gardener's taste.

## POTATO

Place an old tuber in the mouth of a jar. When in doubt as to which end to plant, lay the tuber on wet moss or peat until it discloses itself. The water should be allowed to cover the tip generously so that the tuber is almost half in and half out of the water but not floating. The water supply must be replenished and the level maintained. The potato can be placed in a dark, cool and airy cupboard (as used for spring bulbs) until the white roots make headway. The plant should then be gradually brought into the light and provided with 2—4 strings up which to climb. The potato should be rationed to 4 shoots at most, the others being pinched out. Once in the light it will grow rapidly and the gardener must see to it that the tendrils do his bidding. This is an urgent climber that will keep him busy; a 2 shoot plant often grows to 6 feet.

## CARROT

The carrot's ferny foliage has given a great deal of pleasure to many and its cultivation is simplicity itself.

The carrot's beard is grown by selecting a fat carrot and cutting it across 3 inches from its base: then scoop out the core until only a shallow shell remains. This, when pierced at either side, can be hung up cradle fashion; the feathery fern will soon sprout from the base of the root and hang down. Keep the cup half filled with water.

As a variation, the cup may be treated as a basket, filled with earth and planted with mustard and cress or nasturtium seed. There are few vegetables as elegant as the carrot.

## MUSTARD AND CRESS

Nothing in my budding gardening days riveted my attention more intently than a square of flannel peppered with mustard and cress. Placed on a saucer, and the flannel kept constantly damp, I watched the sprouting. The lightning speed of growth holds the attention of both adult and child alike.

## OTHERS

Horse-radish and beet (with lovely red veining) have their admirers. They should be cut back to 1—2 inches of their roots, and then planted in water and pebbles (in the same way as the paper white narcissi), or in a sandy compost. The finely shaped leaf of the horse-radish is a gay green.

The climbing or runner bean should be planted 2—3 inches deep in pots or trough, about 6 inches apart, sticks or strings fixed in place at the time of planting. Water regularly, feed with Liquinure weekly.

▶ MUSTARD AND CRESS — *will grow with lightning speed on a square of damp flannel, kept moist.*

# ACKNOWLEDGEMENTS

The Author and Publishers would like to thank the following for their help in supplying photographs for this book :

BERNARD ALFIERI LTD.—black and white, pages 17 bottom, 46, 73, 84, 88 top, 100 right, 112, 114, 123, 124 top, centre left and right, 125 centre, 126 centre, 139, 140, 146.

CAMERA PRESS.—colour, page 117 top right.

P. R. CHAPMAN.—black and white, pages 14, 36 top, centre left and right, 115 top, colour, page 118 bottom.

ROBERT CORBIN.—black and white, pages 16, 17 top, 31 top right and bottom, 33, 36 bottom, 37, 43 top, 47, 49, 50, 51, 53, 71 top, 147 top and centre.

J. E. DOWNWARD.—black and white, pages 67, 69, 70, 72, 80, 92, 129, 133 bottom left, 141 right, 143, colour page 135.

FLEETWAY PUBLICATIONS.—black and white, pages 31 top left, 42 bottom, 43 bottom, 45, colour, page 117 top left.

HOME GARDENER.—black and white, pages 7, 9, 30 top.

PETER HUNT.—black and white, pages 11 top, 15, 30 bottom, 42 top, colour, page 165.

R. A. MALBY LIMITED.—black and white, pages 10, 82 bottom, 147 bottom.

MURPHY CHEMICAL CO. LIMITED.—black and white; pages 55 bottom, 60 bottom.

RADIO TIMES HULTON PICTURE LIBRARY.—black and white, page 34.

THOMAS ROCHFORD & SONS LIMITED.—Colour, frontispiece, pages 57 top, 58 top, 96 top, 117 bottom.

SHELL INTERNATIONAL PETROLEUM LIMITED.—black and white, pages 55 top, 60 top.

ANTHEA SIEVEKING—black and white, pages 24 top and bottom right, 26, 27.

H. SMITH.—colour, pages 39, 57 bottom, 75, 96 bottom, 136, black and white, pages 66, 71 bottom, 88 bottom, 90, 115 bottom, 124 bottom, 125 top and bottom, 126 bottom and right, 127, 133 top.

SYNDICATION INTERNATIONAL.—black and white, pages 81, 85, 87, 111, 133 bottom right, 138 bottom, 141 left, 144 bottom.

C. W. TEAGER.—black and white, pages 11 bottom, 13, 29, 44, 61, 63, 64, 65 bottom, 82 top, 83, 89, 93, 97, 99, 101, 102, 103, 110, 113, 121, 122 bottom, 126 top, 128, 138 top, 149.

FRONT COVER.

CAMERA PRESS—centre left.

P. R. CHAPMAN.—top centre.

THOMAS ROCHFORD & SONS LIMITED.—centre right.

H. SMITH.—top left and right, bottom left, centre and right.

# INDEX